MW00466400

ORGANIZING
you

ORGANIZING
YOU

Finding Your Spiritual Clutter and
Using Organization to Clear It Out

SHANNON UPTON

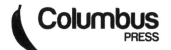

Columbus Press
P.O. Box 91028
Columbus, OH 43209
www.ColumbusPressBooks.com

EDITORS
Brad Pauquette & Emily Hitchcock

ARTWORK, DESIGN & PRODUCTION
Columbus Publishing Lab
www.ColumbusPublishingLab.com

Paperback ISBN 978-1-63337-070-8
Ebook ISBN 978-1-63337-084-5

Printed in the United States of America
1 3 5 7 9 10 8 6 4 2

Organizing You

Contents

Chapter 1: Building Your House   3

Chapter 2: Having a Plan   21

Chapter 3: Getting Stuff Done—and Enjoying It!   40

Chapter 4: Chores   61

Chapter 5: The Big Five   79

Chapter 6: Chores, Again   102

Chapter 7: Planning for Fun   118

Chapter 8: Loving Lists   139

Chapter 9: Fun and Jesus Lists   158

Chapter 10: An Uncluttered Spirit   178

Afterword   197

About the Author   201

Study Guide: Steps along the Journey   203

Appendixes

    Appendix A: Prayerful Planning   227

    Appendix B: Example Goals   230

    Appendix C: Your Daily Planning Space   236

    Appendix D: Chore Card Ideas   238

    Appendix E: Monthly List Examples   243

    Appendix F: Scriptures   248

To honor my God

And to honor my mom, a beautiful, amazing Jesus Mom

Chapter 1

Building Your House

So how organized *are* you?

Maybe you're a really organized person, and you pick up books like this hoping for some fun tips to make your household run a little smoother. Maybe you're a woman who's not totally satisfied with the state of her home, and you're hoping for some inspiration to get you going. Or maybe you're a mom who's looking at the utter chaos surrounding her, thinking, *I hope this book can help me crawl out of this mess.*

The good news is, it doesn't matter which of those women you are. This book isn't really about that. I'm not going to tell you how to "get organized" with some rigid system you'll never be able to sustain. I'm not going to give you any quick fixes to help you "get by" without going crazy, either. Jesus didn't save us so we could struggle with perfection, or merely survive this precious time with our kids at home! He came so that we could have life, and have it *abundantly*.

An abundant life in Christ doesn't require perfectly organized closets filled with neatly labeled boxes, or even a fabulous, color-coded family schedule. I asked a misleading question up there. Whether you love being organized or struggle with structure, the real question this book challenges you to answer is this: how organized are *you*?

No matter how organized—or disorganized—your home is, you have a separate, inner sense of how organized *you* are. Yes, you want your household to be functionally organized, but even more, you want to feel the peace that comes when you have things running smoothly. As a mom, you want to feel organized enough to really enjoy the family God has given you; as a Christian, you strive to grow closer to Jesus and live in His joy.

Well, get ready. You're about to take a deeply faith-driven journey toward a down-to-earth, Jesus perspective on running your home. As you read, you'll learn to view organization, not as an end unto itself, but as a tool to help you clear out the clutter in your mind and heart. Slowly but surely, you'll be eradicating *spiritual clutter*—the white noise of negative thoughts and fears that keeps us distracted from our families and distanced from God.

So often we mothers walk through life hurried, hassled, and distracted, our hearts filled with worry and our minds cluttered with to-do lists. Have you ever been carrying a load of laundry up the stairs and paused impatiently while your child tried to show you a crayon masterpiece? I know I have, and then felt guilty about my attitude afterwards. When I'm trying to load the dishwasher and my husband pins me in a surprise hug, I'll admit that sometimes I feel my frustration more than his love.

When I don't stop to fully appreciate these moments, I imagine God shaking His head and saying with a sigh, "Oh, my daughter, you missed it." God didn't lovingly create us so we would scurry around like ants, feeling uptight and stressed out. He gave us beautiful lives filled with moments to cherish. It breaks my heart to think of all the blessings we're missing in our quest to be great moms and runners of households.

After all, it's an awesome, meaningful mission! Wonderful, loving homes don't just happen—we moms have to be intentional about making them happen. We read books like this because we know we need to be somewhat organized in order to build the homes our families deserve.

But while we're doing our best to stay organized and on top of things, our spirits can become more cluttered than our coffee tables. We have so many blessings we stress ourselves out trying to discern how to make the most of them! When we try to "get organized" in order to reach our own unrealistic expectations, we're bound to miss the point: Jesus. What our husbands and kids really need is a mom living in the abundance of Christ, not a "supermom."

Supermom (ugh)

You know Supermom—at least your version of her. In my mind's eye, Supermom has a gorgeously decorated, immaculately clean home, with a place for everything and everything in its place. She is beautifully groomed, and her kids are always dressed and pressed and perfectly behaved, engaged in some kind of brain-stimulating activity. While supervising the kids (and the dinner in the oven), she's diligently working on some kind of Christian charity work. Her husband finds her to be a competent partner, a sympathetic listening ear, and a great cook. And dare I say sexy? Now, *she* is organized, right?

Organized, and really superficial. Supermom's all about appearances. There's no guarantee that her "success" gives her happiness, and she certainly doesn't sound very fun to hang out with! The fact is, we can organize our homes until each and every item has those neat little labels I mentioned, and we still wouldn't be the perfect supermom. There's no such thing as "perfect" unless you're Jesus, and let's face it, we aren't!

Here's where I have to admit to being a recovering perfectionist, a first-born kid with a Type A personality. Part of me would love to be Supermom…or at least like Mary Poppins, Practically Perfect in Every Way. I'm the kind of mom who struggles with the tendency to pick up my kids' toys while they're still playing with them. At a church potluck, I want to have the best dish in the food line and the best-behaved kids sitting at the table (with my sweet husband, Travis, at my side, saying I look skinny today and so I should absolutely go get some of that chocolate dessert).

Of course, the Lord knows all about my control-seeking heart, and several years ago He started a great work in my life to help me change for the better. So before you start thinking, *Oh no, she's one of* those *moms. I'm not going to be able to learn anything from her*, let me tell you a little story.

How this book was born (and Oliver, too)

After my daughter, Karly, was born, I developed a postpartum anxiety disorder. Postpartum anxiety is much like postpartum depression, but instead of being sad all the time, I was scared all the time. Suddenly, I was living in a perpetual state of panic, and the control I thought I had over my life was gone.

I was afraid to leave the house, afraid to climb stairs, afraid to eat things I thought might choke me. I was afraid to see my family and friends, or even talk to them on the phone, because then they would know I was going crazy. Above all things, I feared for Karly's life, and for the life of my older son, Spencer. I became convinced that if I didn't give Spencer and Karly my constant, vigilant attention, they would die and it would be *my fault*.

By the time Karly was just a few days old, I knew something was very, very wrong with me, and I sought help. I saw a therapist and then a psychiatrist, trying different behavioral modifications and medications without much success. And I prayed—a lot.

I gave my fear to God day after day. I asked Him to protect my home and my kids from the spirit of fear that filled me. At first I prayed for healing, but after a time I began to ask for clarity and wisdom instead. I opened my heart, trying to understand why God was allowing me to have such a horrible experience. And I clung to His promise that He works *all things* for good, even this short-term time of misery.

I mean, it had to be short-term, right? I assumed that after nine months or so, my postpartum time would be over and the anxiety would fade away…but I was wrong. Karly turned one year old, and then eighteen months old, and then two, and yet every day brought a new struggle against irrational worries. I began to realize that I wasn't just trusting God with my fears until the anxiety disorder ran its course—I was trusting Him to help the new, anxious me live a life that would glorify Him *regardless* of my fears.

Then, while pregnant with my third child, the Holy Spirit inspired me to pray with renewed fervor that the Lord would lift the burden. Each day I prayed for the baby to grow healthy, strong, and happy…and then I prayed for the healing of my spirit. I prayed that God would be gracious enough to use those special nine months to reset in my body whatever had gone out of whack in my last pregnancy.

My husband, parents, and friends all lovingly told me that I shouldn't get my hopes up, and I agreed with them. My psychiatrist politely listened about my prayers, and then gently told me that he had never heard of a pregnancy being curative for an anxiety disorder—in fact, pregnancies usually make things worse. I told him that I understood and would keep it in mind, but I still prayed.

Every time I prayed I told God that I knew He *could* heal me, I just didn't know if He *would*. If He didn't, then I would accept it as part of His plan and design for my life. But I had so much hope.

Almost four years to the day after Karly was born, little Oliver entered the world and I knew God had healed me. In the hospital I was cautiously optimistic, those first few weeks at home I was just plain optimistic, and by the time Oliver was a few months old I was jubilant! Our Lord, who is gracious and mighty and merciful, gave me such an amazing spiritual blessing. He lifted that constant, irrational fear from my heart, and I will be thankful and grateful to Him forever.

Now *that* mom has it together. Doesn't she?

Now, this doesn't mean my life is anxiety-free. I still have days when my heart races and I worry that a bad moon is risin'. I know I had these moments before I'd ever heard of an anxiety disorder, before I became a mom, even before I became an official grown-up. But because God allowed me to have that horrible clinical anxiety experience, I learned to recognize these fears for what they are: irrational and baseless.

During my anxiety struggle, my fears were constantly shouting at me, *SOMETHING IS WRONG! YOU ARE NOT OK!* Those thoughts were urgent and overwhelming, often paralyzing me into inaction or sending me off into panic attacks. Now I've realized that those feelings stemmed from more pedestrian, subtle feelings of inadequacy. Those thoughts haven't gone away, oh no—they're just more insidious.

As I reached out to other women during my time of deep anxiety, God revealed to me that this kind of thinking is sadly prevalent in the hearts of Christian moms. One by one, the caring women with whom I shared my troubles empathetically told me about the similar fears they face. We all have irrational thoughts and fears that keep us from being the women of God we want to be, even if we don't always consciously recognize it as the spiritual clutter it is.

We find ourselves thinking that we should be doing this *better*, that we should be better moms and wives and daughters of God. We worry that things aren't quite right, that we're not doing this whole mom thing the way we should be. Are we letting down our families? Or worse, our Lord?

In one of my first tentative forays into social life after Karly was born, I made a new friend named Tara and invited her and her kids over for a playdate. I had the kids do a craft together, and then got out some fun toys. I made a simple pasta lunch that I thought both the kids and the moms would enjoy. I asked Tara great questions about her husband, her kids, and her career.

In short, I tried very hard to let go of my anxieties and appear as though I were a "normal" mom who had things together like Tara and my other friends did. And it was working—I thought the playdate was going really well. Then I noticed that there was a knife out on the counter, and that little Karly was toddling around just a few feet away.

Now, rest assured that Karly was nowhere close to the counter, and she couldn't possibly have reached that knife even if she'd wanted to. My head knew that, but my heart didn't. Tara saw my obvious panic as I quickly moved the knife to the relative safety of the sink (and then, after a moment's hesitation, into the even safer dishwasher). She would've let it pass, but in the spirit of new friendship I briefly shared that I was struggling with an anxiety disorder, my main fear being that something would happen to Karly.

I was in the early stages of sharing this with friends and had received mixed reactions, ranging from empathetic to curious. I was unprepared for Tara's reaction, though. Her shoulders drooped as she sighed with relief and said, "Well, there you go. Everyone has something, don't they? Nobody's *perfect*." As she said "perfect," she made a sweeping gesture with her hand that seemed to indicate my house, my kids, and me. (It was at this point I realized I might've overdone the playdate just a bit.)

Tara's reaction just underscored for me how we moms tend to compare ourselves to each other. Other moms seem to have it "together"—wasn't that the standard I was trying so hard to meet by hosting the perfect playdate? We see other moms doing their jobs seemingly without effort, and deep down in our hearts, we suspect that we don't measure up.

We all hear those thoughts telling us that we should be doing our jobs as mom and wife and homemaker better. And while striving to be better is good and worthwhile, striving to be perfect isn't. No mom is Supermom. We need a more realistic goal, a different finish line to strive for as we run this mommy race for our families and for God.

The Jesus Mom

So instead of the Supermom, let's try to picture the Jesus Mom, a what-would-Jesus-do woman who's doing her best for her family. She's a modern-day Proverbs 31 gal, working hard in the home and possibly out of it (though probably without servants). She runs an efficient yet relaxed household for herself, her husband, and her kids. She's organized, but balanced. Her home isn't spotless, but it is clean and tidy. You can feel the warmth and love when you walk through her door.

She doesn't hurry through life, but she and her family members are usually on time and prepared for whatever's next. Her husband wants to be home more than he wants to be anywhere else, and he's proud of her for the wonderful job she's doing with the home they're building together. Her kids understand structure and feel stable at home. They can always feel just how much they are loved, because the love of God is purposefully woven through every moment of their days.

The Jesus Mom is filled with peace that things in her home are running smoothly. Her chores get done, she remembers appointments and her friends' birthdays, and she's spending her time on things that are important to her. Best of all, her spirit is peaceful enough to feel the presence of the Lord throughout her day. She is using every aspect of her life to bring glory to Christ her Savior.

Hopefully, there are parts of my Jesus Mom description that resonate with you. When you picture her, your image will probably be a bit different than mine. The Jesus Mom is not cookie-cutter, and she's not perfect either. The Lord's grace covers her imperfections, because the Jesus Mom lives with intention. She does her best for her family and her God, and her heart is satisfied.

Your heart can be satisfied as well. Whatever she looks like to you, you *can* become a Jesus Mom. In fact, since you're loving your family with the love of God, you already are one—your spirit may just be too cluttered with stress and worry to realize it. You're a *great* mom, and when you use organization to clear out your spiritual clutter, you'll be an even better one.

Being organized or "together" isn't an inborn talent, it's a skill you can learn. With prayer and consideration, you *can* make your home run smoothly—most of the time!—and clear those negative, worrisome thoughts out of your spirit. You can cultivate an organized lifestyle that works for you and your family, one that's just organized enough for you to be filled with God's peace.

Just who's in charge here?

Our goal is to gain that sense of peace by choosing to live a more organized life, but as we embark on this journey, we should talk about control. We are The Moms, the runners of our households, and we make innumerable decisions each day about how the members of our family live their lives. This is our one chance at life, our children's one chance to grow up, and we don't want to blow it. So we get organized, trying to take control of everything that might affect our family's well-being.

When we take all that responsibility upon ourselves, we clutter up our own spirits. We need to take a few minutes to acknowledge that a lot of life is out of our control, and that's the way it should be. We're The Moms, but we are not God.

He is the ultimate Lord of our homes, and *real* peace comes from understanding that He is infinitely more organized than we are. We can rest in the fact that while we're being good stewards with what we're given, God has it all under His control. He's guiding our lives and holding our families lovingly in His hands.

An organized lifestyle doesn't give Jesus Moms more control, it helps us to grow closer to the Lord. When you clear out your spiritual clutter, you'll be able to feel His leading and guidance as you make all those decisions, large and small, that affect your family. You'll be more open to His quiet whisper throughout the day. You'll let go of your worries about the little things and focus on the bigger picture: the Heavenly rewards of running your household in an organized, Jesus Mom way. Yes, there are some!

When we think about our jobs as Christian moms, we tend to go a little extreme. Either we get stuck in the earthly expectation of supermom perfection, or we take the "eternal perspective" and worry that our work isn't making an impact for the Kingdom of God. When we get to Heaven, will it really matter how healthily we packed our kids' lunches? Does Jesus care how clean our floors are?

Well, in a way, yes! With a heart focused on God, keeping house isn't just a set of simple and repetitive tasks. With every completed chore, we're building the spirit and life of our homes. We spend our days inspiring faith in our children, and building relationships with others so we can do the same for them.

Now, I know you're thinking, *Come on, Shannon, I spend my days cleaning potties and doing laundry.* Sometimes those mundane tasks can seem fruitless. Mopping the kitchen floor doesn't seem very heavenly, especially the minute your kids walk across it with muddy shoes. And every mom has had the experience (and if you haven't, then you will) of tucking that last bit of clean laundry into a drawer, and then having your kid throw up on something. Your sense of accomplishment fades into the realization that you're going to have to throw in another load...and another, and another, forever and ever, Amen.

Jesus Moms, God sees us and knows us. The work we do *matters* to Him, and He's called us to do that work for the love of Him. When we take out the trash (again) with the happiest hearts we can muster, Jesus feels our love for Him and for our families.

God cherishes us and is greatly pleased with the work we do as mothers and homemakers.

As Christian mothers, we choose to build our homes for our families and dedicate all our labors, no matter how small, to the Lord. And as we endeavor to please Him, we can use organization as a means to be good stewards with what He's given us and grow closer to Him. *This* is how God wants us to live our lives—I think He even told us so.

Ye shall be organized

OK, so the Bible doesn't actually say, "Ye shall be organized," not even in the King James Version. However, our God *is* a God of Order.

As a math nerd, I can attest to this. I studied pure mathematics in college, and I was constantly awed by the order in our universe, especially how certain ratios and number sequences occur in nature again and again. Studying number theory only made me more certain that there is a God, and that He created our world in an amazingly structured, logical way. The more I learned, the more I discovered that our God is a God of Order.

When Paul wrote his first letter to the Corinthians, he addressed the fact that their worship time had gotten out of hand, with people speaking over each other because everyone wanted to have their say. So he gave them instructions for fitting, orderly worship (how very organized of him!), and told them this truth:

> For God is not a God of disorder but of peace.
>
> *I Corinthians 14:33*

Disorder in our lives is counterproductive to peace in our hearts. Our God is a God of Order, and He created us to be this way as well. He wants to bless us with a spirit of peace, but our chaos and disorder get in the way. Instead, we can intentionally use organization to settle our hearts so that we grow closer to the Lord and our families.

Though the Bible doesn't have much to say about home organization, there is the book of Proverbs, which is filled with pertinent advice. Proverbs 14:1 is specifically addressed to us, the women who run our households:

> The wise woman builds her house,
> but with her own hands the foolish one tears hers down.
>
> *Proverbs 14:1*

I don't know about you, but I shudder at the thought of being the foolish woman. Take a step back and think about how you're building your house. Are you the wise woman, or is there a part of you tearing things down? That can be a scary question, but Proverbs 14 also says:

The wisdom of the prudent is to give thought to their ways.

Proverbs 14:8a

As you read this book, my challenge to you is to give some thought to your ways and build your house with both hands. We're going to take a journey with Jesus, a deep-thinking look at how you do the things you do…and why. We're going to look at your time and to-do lists and chores and very *thoughts* in the light of Heaven. We're going to discover all of the various things that clutter up your spirit, and use organization and right thinking to get rid of them.

Go ahead and grab a notebook and pen to keep alongside this book. As you're reading, sometimes you'll feel challenged and convicted that you need to make some changes, and you'll want to take some notes. Sometimes you'll feel affirmed about what you're already doing, and you'll want to apply those things to more areas of your life. You'll find some great ideas here, and you'll think of new ideas that suit your individual lifestyle and needs—write everything down so it doesn't end up as even more spiritual clutter!

If you do want to try out my way of organizing (obviously,

I think I have some pretty great systems for you), check out the **Steps along the Journey** study guide at the end of the book. The questions and suggested activities there will help you consider how things are for you right now, and how you'd like to change them. If you'd like the support of friends, host an Organizing *You* Group Bible Study.[1]

Just keep in mind you don't have to organize *exactly* my way—in fact, you probably won't! Instead, you'll be discerning what kinds of systems will work for you and your family. Honestly reflect, prayerfully plan, and organize *you*.

This is a faith-driven book. I truly believe the Lord led me to write it in order to help you clear out the clutter in your spirit, and organize your household while you're at it. My prayer is that the Holy Spirit will guide you as you build a better home for your family, growing closer to them and closer to Jesus.

So let's get started building your house!

---

1 The curriculum is free through OrganizingJesusMoms.com. Yes, free!

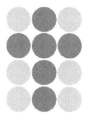

Chapter 2

Having a Plan

Let's start with your time.

Time management is the cornerstone of all organization—after all, how can you clean out that closet if you can't figure out when to do it? And in terms of spiritual clutter, few things keep your mind and heart more troubled than that persistent feeling of being too overwhelmed to get to the things that matter in your life.

As mothers, our time is invaluable. Impressive lawyers charge hundreds of dollars an hour to serve their clients, but we're so very important we don't even *get* paid. Let's face it, no one could afford us. We're *raising children*, furthering the Kingdom of God, doing some of the best work there is. And at some point, we've got to find the time to clean the bathrooms.

All moms are "in demand," and there may be a part of you that enjoys it. You may think you're more productive when you feel a built-up sense of pressure. You may like being overwhelmed with things to do because it gives you a false sense of purpose and worth. Being the busiest mom on the block (or at least tied for the title) may make you feel important—when it's not making you feel crazy and out of control.

Even if being stressed-out busy has its rewards for you, chances are your loved ones don't enjoy it in the same way. Your friends, who patiently listen to you talk about how stressed and busy you are, may wish you'd do something about it. Your husband and kids may yearn for a more relaxed pace and a less overwhelmed you. How do you think God views your busyness?

If you're keeping up the fastest pace you can possibly stand, then you're cluttering up your own spirit and tearing down your household, guaranteed. You're majoring in the minors, choosing lots of good but missing the best. You need to take a look at how you're using your time.

You've heard it said that we all have twenty-four hours a day, it's just a matter of how we use it. Well, that's true, and then it isn't. Everyone has the same number of hours in a day, but we all have different responsibilities and constraints on our time. Some of us have kids with health problems that necessitate time spent at several doctors' appointments a week. Some of us have kids who aren't sleeping through the night, which changes the entire *feel* of time. Some of us have a full-time job and ten kids (although if you do, I don't know how you're making the time to read this).

No matter what the demands on our time are, all moms are busy. It's just a given. We don't want to compare ourselves to others, awed at what they get done or jealous about what they get to do. We need to look at our own time constraints and decide to choose what's best for us: what God wants for our lives.

As Jesus Moms, we recognize that our sense of importance, worth, and purpose come only from God, and we deeply appreciate that our time here is a precious gift from Him. But when we're not careful, the things He calls us to do with our time can get pushed aside. The things we *want* to do can get buried under the things we feel we *have* to do. We need time management skills to make sure we're spending our time on what's important to us, our families, and our Lord. We need a plan.

The sheer joy of a daily planner

Now, don't be scared by the word "planner." You already do a certain amount of daily planning. No matter how unorganized you are, you generally have a loose plan in mind each day, even if it's in the form of a big fat mental to-do list or a bunch of Post-it notes filled with random things you don't want to forget. We're just going to take it up a notch (or two) in order to get you living your priorities.

Without a doubt, the best way to organize time is with a daily planner. I strongly recommend getting one that works for you. There aren't very many organizational systems I would recommend for every mom, but I truly feel that *every* mom would benefit from the flexible use of a daily planner. Yes, that means *you*.

If you're feeling resistant, do me a favor and try to keep reading with an open mind. If you already have a planner, you should keep reading, too. You may discover new ideas—ways to use it to its full potential. You might even decide to try out a different planner system.

There are many great planners out there to choose from, and any planner at all can help you. My very first planner was a college student one, formatted mostly to keep track of classes and assignments. Besides jotting down a couple of important dates, that's all I really used it for. I thought "real" planners were for business people (like those important lawyers I mentioned).

Fresh out of college, I found a teaching job at a local high school and began to eagerly anticipate my first day of school as Miss Kelley, Math Teacher Extraordinaire. When I heard that my school district was sponsoring a workshop about time management the day before school started, I decided to go. Why not start the year by earning some Continuing Education Units? Not only would I work toward renewing my teaching certificate before I'd even started teaching, but I might learn something fun! (Did I mention that I used to be really Type-A?)

The workshop was given by the Franklin Covey company, and it made me into a Franklin Planner Girl. I received a small binder with a neat stack of planner pages to put in it. Each page was covered with little lines and spaces to fill out in perfectionist form. My excitement grew as I listened to the engaging, knowledgeable presenter tell us how to use our planners successfully. When I left, my head was spinning with the new time management skills I'd learned. I had glimpsed organizational bliss.

That seminar shaped my teaching career more than any other educational conference I attended. The perfectionism didn't last long, and over time I came up with different, looser systems of my own (which I will pass on to you), but in that conference, I learned how to effectively organize my time. Each year I taught, I bought the refill pack of planner pages and considered it money well-spent.

Then I became pregnant with Spencer, decided to be a stay-at-home mom, and thought I didn't need a planner any more. Why would I, being at home all day? What would I write in it, "load the dishwasher" or "change the stinky diaper"? I placed my planner in a drawer and started decorating the nursery.

As I'm sure you've guessed, after Spencer was born, I got

a well-deserved kick in the pants. I quickly realized that being a mom is *very* demanding on your time, and asked my husband to put those planner page refills back into our budget. I needed them like I never had before, and as we added Karly and Oliver into the mix, things just ramped up—in a fantastic way!

Being a mom involves more planning than I had thought possible. Jesus Moms need a planner to keep track of our responsibilities and projects. We deserve a place to write down our goals and our thoughts. Piles of paper on a counter are not good enough for us, the Builders of our Homes! So if you don't have a planner, or think you might want to choose a better one, now's the time to go for it.

On OrganizingJesusMoms.com, I offer free Organizing *You* planner pages that go hand-in-hand with the Organizing *You* books. To use these printable pages, all you'll need is paper, a 3-hole punch, a 3-ring binder, and tabbed divider pages. I would absolutely love for you to use that resource to manage your time to its fullest! They're the pages I use and I love them. (Almost as much as I love chocolate—they're that good.)

If you'd rather shop for a planner, be sure to spend the extra money for a planning system that includes a binder with rings and refill pages. You'll also want to have separate sections in the back for lists and notes (we'll discuss those lists later). Look for daily pages, not a weekly view. And don't go small—you'll want to have plenty of room to write without making your own handwriting too hard to read.

You may notice that I'm talking about actual paper here and ignoring the whole computer/cell phone thing... I know. I'll talk more about my lack of technology love a little later when it's even more disconcerting to you. For now, I'm going to write about paper planners, and if you want to, you can apply the ideas to your favorite program or app.

I'd still love for you to give the actual paper a try first. The free Organizing *You* pages should certainly fit in your budget! You can even design a daily page layout on your computer and print out a month's worth at a time. (If you choose this option, you should also buy tabbed dividers to keep the list sections in the back separate from your daily pages.) Your planner doesn't have to be fancy, just be sure to get one!

Setting goals (it's not that hard)

You'll be writing lots of things in your planner. Things you need to do, things you want to remember—anything that's important for you to have written down in order to clear out the jumble of "should" and "have to" thoughts in your mind. A clean, fresh planner is exciting, but it's hard to know where to begin. Since you're a Jesus Mom giving thought to her ways, I encourage you to start by turning to the blank pages at the back of your planner and writing down your goals.

So go on, write your goals now.

How are they looking?

Faced with a blank piece of paper, you may have trouble coming up with a beautiful, worthy list of goals. If so, that's very un-American. Just kidding. I'll admit that I generally dislike these "self-help" kinds of exercises, and often skip over them. I always feel such pressure to have spectacular goals that I can't seem to think of any, anyway.

Jesus Moms, don't skip this part! The first step to clearing out your spiritual clutter is figuring out what's really important to you. What is it that you want to do in this life—and are you doing it? If great goals aren't springing to mind, I have some things for you to consider.

If someone asked me to tell them the Point of Life in Ten Words or Less, I would say that we're here to love God and love each other. Even more concise: Life is about relationships. The work we do to build our relationships with the Lord and with other believers is work with eternal significance, because we'll continue those relationships in Heaven. And the work we put into our re-lationships with nonbelievers is incredibly significant because of the impact we hope to make: we want to see them in Heaven, too.

Jesus Moms, we can be a huge force for the Lord when it comes to the people in our lives. You can identify plenty of specific goals by considering the current state of your relationships. What can you do to forge stronger bonds with the ones you love?

First, we're daughters of God, beloved by Him, and He wants us to be in an intimate relationship with Him. Although our relationship with God is paramount, our time with Him often takes a backseat to the things that "need" to get done. What's a goal you can set that will bring you a step closer to Him? Feel free to stop right now and ask Him to whisper His advice into your heart. Your goal may be to read the Bible each day, spend more time in prayer, spend time in personal worship, or anything else that the Lord lays on your heart.

If you're married, your relationship with your husband is the next one to consider. What can you do to help him feel your love? What will draw you closer together? Maybe you want to be more physically affectionate, surprise him by helping out with his chores, buy him little gifts, plan date nights, or remember to write him little love notes. (Reading these five suggestions, you may be able to tell that I am a *big* fan of Gary Chapman's *The Five Love Languages*. If you haven't read it, well, there's a goal for you!)

The next people you need to consider are little ones: your kids. Even if your children are bigger than you (or maybe especially if they are), you need to keep your relationships with them strong. The mothering instinct is a powerful gift from God, and with a little thought and prayer, you may feel the need to set a certain mothering goal. You'll probably want to write a different goal for each of your children according to their specific needs so you can better connect with them individually.

You may even want to ask your husband and kids what goals *they* would set for you as you strive to be a better wife and mother. (But only ask them if you're actually ready to hear their answers—they may give you some real food for thought!) You can also set goals that are specifically aimed at shaping your family into a tighter unit. As moms, we can encourage our kids to strengthen their relationships with their dad and with each other by setting family goals that will help the members of your household grow closer to each other and to the Lord.

As with your children, you'll want to consider your relationships with your extended family members and friends individually. Some of those relationships are in a purely fun place, so making a goal to schedule a "girl time" outing may be the perfect way to strengthen a friendship. Others may be in need of some help or support you could give. Pursuing a goal to support these people will draw you closer to them, and closer to the Lord as you work in His service.

And speaking of His service, Christ's great commission to us was to go and make disciples, so look around your life for unbelievers. How can you strengthen your relationships with them so you can be an effective witness for the Lord? Whom do you need to invite to church with you? Whom do you need to invite out to coffee so you can share your testimony? Who needs loving care before they can even begin to hear the words you want to share? In this, as in all of your goal setting, ask the Holy Spirit to guide you.

We can intentionally use the precious gift of our time to show Jesus to people who don't even know they're looking for Him, and to be a blessing and support for our Christian brothers and sisters. As you consider the people in your life—family and friends, coworkers and acquaintances, believers and nonbelievers—decide what you want to do to strengthen your relationships and further the Kingdom of God here on Earth. Look at them with Christ's love and decide to make an eternal impact with the time He's given you.

That awesome woman of God—you

All of this brings us to the one person you haven't considered when goal writing. It's time to think about *you*—you as a person. What goals do you have for yourself? What goals does God have for you? How can you bring Him glory?

Do you have projects you want to complete at work or at

home? What are the places you want to see and things you want to learn? Do you want to be healthier in some way? Is there a habit you want to get into, or an attitude you'd like to cultivate? Is there a ministry you'd like to support with your efforts? Do you have a passion, a calling from the Lord? This is your time to write down all of those ideas in the form of actual goals.

As you consider the woman of God you want to be, you may hear some of those bothersome, negative thoughts telling you that you aren't good enough, that you aren't being a good steward of what God has given you. That spiritual clutter can clog up your thoughts, and for once, it's OK. You can use that mess to make some of your goals take shape.

If you find yourself thinking, *I should play with the kids more*, you might need to write a goal about spending time with your kids. But really think about what you and your kids need. What's the best way for you to make connections with them? How much will be "enough"? What's a realistic goal for you and for them?

Or maybe you've recently visited a friend's house and thought, *Wow, her house looks great—my house is a mess*. Realistically speaking, your friend probably spent some time cleaning up before you came over, so don't be too hard on yourself. But that negative thought should prompt you to consider: just how clean does your house need to be to satisfy you? Are your standards too high, or too low? Is it really cleanliness you're thinking of, or is it just neatness?

When you're writing goals for yourself, listen for your dreams and your anxious thoughts. Then finish up with this question: How do you see yourself being a Jesus Mom? How do you envision the woman God wants you to be?

And, how in the world are you going to accomplish all this?

Procrastinating, in a good way

You may be thinking, *I can't believe she's giving me* more *to do. How's this going to help me clear the huge pile of stuff off my dining room table?* The immediate answer is, it won't...but it might make that pile of stuff matter to you a little less.

You're doing even better work: clearing the pile of nagging thoughts out of your spirit. As you start working toward your goals (and clearing off that table might be one of them!), you'll be focusing on the things that really matter instead of being distracted by the less important things that clutter your mind. Are you ready for some of that relief?

It's time to take a look at your big, stellar list of goals and break them up a bit. First of all, set aside all the goals that have to do with chores: those things we do day after day, week after week, year after year. Things like cleaning, laundry, watering your plants so they don't die, and changing the batteries in your smoke detectors so you don't die. Chores take up a lot of a mom's time, so goals about doing them are fantastic. We're definitely going to talk about them later on, but for now, set them aside.

Your remaining list should be filled with personal goals and project-oriented goals. Next you need to weed out the goals that are less important and not as time-sensitive. You're going to move them onto what I call The Greater To-Do List. It's a constantly growing, shrinking, and evolving list of stuff that you *do* want to do…someday.

Greater To-Do List items are important, but not urgent. I keep mine in the back of my planner, right behind my Goal List. My Greater To-Do List has all kinds of goals reflected on it, from things that I want to do with my family this summer to things I hope to do after my kids are all in school. I even have a few things I want to do as an empty nester.

I want to make homemade Christmas tags with a friend this summer, before we get too busy with other holiday chores. I want to choose some new family room furniture when we've made room in our budget, hopefully next year. I want to volunteer at the kids' school more when Oliver is a little older. I want to learn to play cribbage because my mom used to play it with her grandfather. I want to take the kids to the Grand Canyon someday. I'm *really* looking forward to doing all of these things—just not today.

You need to write down your long-term goals and plans in order to keep them from cluttering your heart with *Don't forget about that* thoughts. After all, they're great goals, or fun goals, or necessary goals you don't want to forget—they just have to wait. Yes, even good things you really want to do or feel you *should* do.

When it's not your time

When I was pregnant with Oliver, I signed up to teach Spencer's Sunday school class until the baby was born. Sadly, I had a tough pregnancy and needed to drop out of all of my activities well before Oliver made his grand entrance. I was sorely disappointed and felt more than a little guilty about backing out of my Sunday morning commitment.

Then, two weeks after Oliver was born, I received a group e-mail from our fabulous, aptly named Children's Activities Director, Joy. She wrote that Karly's Sunday school teacher was going to be absent the following Sunday, and all of the class parents were asked to consider volunteering to sub. I jumped at the chance and replied to Joy that I could do it—I just needed to double check with Travis, because the kids had colds (including tiny Oliver), which meant Daddy would need to stay home alone with all three of them on Sunday morning.

Before I could check with Travis, my in-box held a reply

from Joy which drove straight to the heart of the matter. It read: *Shannon, absolutely not. You will help in your time but THIS IS NOT YOUR TIME. Take care of your baby and your family. Joy*

I cried when I read that e-mail. You remember what life is like two weeks after a new baby joins your family. I was exhausted and worried about Oliver's cold and overwhelmed with life. I wasn't prepared to teach a group of three and four-year-olds that Sunday. And before I knew it, Joy had known it…and it was OK. It was not my time.

I really did want to help with Karly's Sunday school class, and I felt like I "should." I said "yes" out of an honest desire to help, with a little guilt mixed in. What I should've done was take the time to pray and see if the Lord was calling me to serve. Clearly, He wasn't.

In Ecclesiastes, wise King Solomon writes to us that:

There is a time for everything,
and a season for every activity under heaven.

Ecclesiastes 3:1

This verse and the ones that follow are frequently quoted, in both Christian and secular circles. You probably have them memorized, if only because The Byrds set them to music in the 1960's. Several of these verses have to do with work: a time to tear down and a time to build, a time to plant and a time to uproot, a time to tear and a time to mend, a time to cast away stones and a time to gather stones together (turn, turn, turn). God is telling us that there *is* a time for everything, just not all at once.

In verse 9, Solomon tells us more about God's intention for work:

> What does the worker gain from his toil? I have seen the burden God has laid on men. He has made everything beautiful in its time. He has also set eternity in the hearts of men; yet they cannot fathom what God has done from beginning to end. I know that there is nothing better for men than to be happy and do good while they live. That everyone may eat and drink, and find satisfaction in all his toil— this is the gift of God.
>
> *Ecclesiastes 3:9-13*

God takes an eternal view on our work and our goals, a view we cannot even begin to grasp. His plan for us is perfect, and He will make all of our efforts beautiful in His time. He doesn't expect us to tackle all of the work He has in mind for us this week. That's His gift to us. He wants us to faithfully follow His call, in *His* time.

Sometimes the Lord *is* calling you to His work now, even if you don't feel ready for the task or you may have to surrender some of your other goals. I'm all for the sacrificial giving of your time and energy when that's what the Lord calls you to do. You can feel it when the Holy Spirit really lays something on your heart, I *deeply* believe that. (Says the Math Girl with three little ones who inexplicably finds herself writing a book.) Without a doubt, respond to His call.

But sometimes, even if our goals are worthy and Christ-centered, we know deep in our hearts that it's not the time for them. We need to limit our activities so we can honor our God-given callings and priorities. We need to say "no" or "not now" to some things so we can live our lives fully in the presence and peace of our Jesus.

We can't do everything at once, and that's just fine, because we have time. We all hope that God will grant us long lives filled with checkmarks on our bucket lists. The goals on your Greater To-Do List will wait for you if they're in God's plan for your life. He knows your heart's desires, and He has His own desires and plans for your future.

Our job is to do what we can with a happy heart and a sense of peace that God is in control of the rest. The most important thing you can do when writing your goals is to consult the Lord about them. How are you going to use your time, your gifts, and your callings to bring the maximum glory to Christ? Spend some time in prayer over your goals, plans, and dreams.[1] Listen for what the Lord lays on your heart, for now and for someday.

Working on your Goal List isn't just a one-time exercise. To keep living your priorities, you should prayerfully re-visit your Goal List and Greater To-Do List a few times a year (more on how to remember to do this is coming up). Each time, be sure to think through the state of your relationships and the other facets of your life to see if any new goals come to light, or if the time has come for some of your Greater To-Do List goals. After that time of reflection, you'll have a new list of current goals to start meeting—and a refreshed sense of energy about meeting them.

So how are those goals looking now? Get excited, Jesus Moms. Your goals are no longer taking up space in your mind and adding worry, insecurity, and frazzle to your heart. You've cleared out some real spiritual clutter by writing down your goals in the back of your planner. Next we'll turn to the daily pages and get ready to take action!

---

1 For some great questions to pray over as you discern what to move to your Greater To-Do List, check out the "Now and Later: Goal Setting" article on OrganizingJesusMoms.com

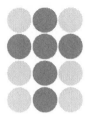

Chapter 3

Getting Stuff Done— and Enjoying It!

Ladies, start your planners. It's time to use organization to make your goals into realities.

You now have a lovely, prayerfully written list of current personal or project-oriented goals, and it may look a little daunting. The key is to take each goal and break it down into steps that can be written on your daily planner pages. Try not to write the whole goal, which is usually non-specific and overwhelming. How would you ever be able to check it off by the end of the day? Decide what you can realistically do today, tomorrow, this weekend, or next week to begin to meet each goal.

Let's start with a project-oriented goal. In the to-do list section on a daily planner page, write the first step you want to take.

After you complete your task, definitely give yourself the small but satisfying experience of checking it off your list. (In my head, the down-up motion of my pen making a checkmark sounds like "uh-*huh!*" How I love it.)

But don't forget to keep working toward that goal! After you make your happy checkmark, immediately turn in your planner to the next day you'll have the opportunity to work toward your goal, and write the next step. Don't let the goal float off the pages of your planner and into your mind, or you'll clutter up your spirit with *I should be working on that* thoughts.

For example, let's say your goal is to throw a baby shower for a friend. Write that on your Goal List at the back of your planner, and then write the first step on today's daily to-do list, maybe "research baby shower ideas online." After you've done your research and formed a clearer picture of the shower you want to throw, check it off your list. You did it!

Right away, turn to the next day you want to work on party preparations and write your next step, "shop @ party store for baby shower items." If you think of more time-sensitive tasks related to the shower, write them on the appropriate daily to-do lists. You might also think of a last-minute task you're afraid you'll forget the day of the party, so flip to that day and write it down there. Try to write neatly, and in clear language, so you'll understand what you wrote in the days and weeks to come.

Once you've written down what you want to remember to do, you can let it go. If overwhelming thoughts about throwing a huge party try to clutter your mind, you can remind yourself that it's all in hand. You're making it happen, and you can forget about it for now and enjoy living your life in the moment. You're doing what you can do and God is in charge of the big picture.

Some of your personal goals may seem harder to break down, like an attitude you'd like to cultivate or a habit you want to get into. I'll be giving you more organizational systems to help you meet your goals in the upcoming chapters (for a sneak peek at how those systems can help you, take a look at Appendix B). For now, start with your daily to-do lists and Family Calendar. Do your best to make it happen!

If you'd like to complain less, try posting Bible verses about complaining tongues by your phone and on your bathroom mirror. Choose a specific time to lift up prayers of gratitude and schedule it on your Family Calendar. Write a to-do item in your planner to greet your husband with a kiss instead of a complaint when he walks through the door. (Yes, you even get to check *that* off—I have checked off lesser things!) Decide to change, and follow through.

You can also utilize the blank memo spaces in your daily planner to help you reach some of your less tangible goals. If you'd like to keep a prayer journal, you can use that easily accessible planner space to write down prayer requests and praises. If you're trying to stick to a budget, you can use the memo space to keep track of your spending.

I'll confess that I almost always use the memo space in my planner to keep track of my "healthy weight" efforts. As long as chocolate is available to me, I will battle the bulge, so I use my planner to help me. Though I don't write daily to-dos about maintaining my weight, every day I use the blank memo space to loosely keep track of what I've eaten and how much I've exercised. If I know that I "have" to write it down, I'm less likely to indulge in an unhealthy snack. And keeping an exercise log helps me feel like I'm really accomplishing something—staying healthy for my husband and kids (and for myself, as well). I need my planner to help me keep track of my efforts and maintain my healthy lifestyle.

How much *you* need to write down in order to meet your goals will vary. If you're skilled at accomplishing your goals without writing down a lot of tasks, then don't make more work for yourself. If you'd rather write a general to-do list in your planner once a week and plug away at it when you've got time, then that's your prerogative. Do what works for you as you strive to meet your goals. And be excited! You're prudently giving thought to your ways, and using time organization to bring yourself closer to your family and to God.

The grand (or not-so-grand) Family Calendar

Daily planners almost always have calendars in them, as well as daily appointment schedules with the hours of the day marching down the page. I never, ever use the calendar in my planner and rarely use the appointment schedules. (If the Franklin Planner seminar instructor heard me say that, I'm sure she'd gasp and be very disappointed in me, but it's true.) For Jesus Moms, time-sensitive tasks and events belong on a Family Calendar.

If you try to use the calendar in your planner in addition to your Family Calendar, two things happen. First, you have to write everything down twice, which is annoying and a total waste of time. Second, you're inviting all kinds of miscommunications. Your husband may write a nighttime business meeting on your Family Calendar, but he almost certainly won't remember to write in your planner, so you'll end up waiting on him for dinner. In a hurry, you may jot a new appointment with the pediatrician in your planner, but forget to write it on your calendar, and miss it.

Daily planner calendars and schedules are meant for individuals, and may be very useful to you in your work setting, but Mom Time is too tightly woven into the fabric of the family to be separated. Preschool schedules, evening work events, ballet classes, soccer games, and school programs all involve you, but should be written on a Family Calendar that *everyone* can access and understand.

I'm sure you've seen those moms with awesomely elaborate calendars and charts. Each family member is represented with a different color of pen. Monday/ Wednesday/ Friday activities are highlighted in green, while Tuesday/Thursday activities are highlighted in blue. It all looks very colorful and impressive. Maybe you're one of those moms, and if it truly works for you, then go with it!

But for most moms, that would be over organizing. You don't need to work so hard to have a great Family Calendar! Why spend time figuring out the right color of pen when you want to jot something down? Why set up a system too complicated for the other members of your family to use? (And won't you know an activity is on Tuesdays without blue highlighter?)

Hang a simple Family Calendar in a central locale that will encourage you and the other members of your family to write on it—probably in your kitchen, the hub of the home. Or you may want to keep it near your computer so it's easy to access as you make appointments and other plans. If you're using an electronic calendar, be sure that your entire family is using the same one.

Your daily planner should also be conveniently located in order to catch the thoughts buzzing around your head. At work, your planner should have a prominent spot on your workspace. At home, it should be where you are most. If an *I should really...*

or an *I've got to remember to…* thought is pestering you, you're more likely to write it down when your planner's handy. In so doing, you've moved one piece of mental clutter into your organizational system, so your heart can let it go.

No matter what, your planner and Family Calendar should be side-by-side. Think of them as BFFs, practically inseparable. That way, when you write an event on the calendar, you can immediately write down any tasks associated with it in your planner. When your child is invited to a birthday party, that's a Family Calendar *and* daily planner event! You should write the date and time of the party on your calendar, then write "buy and wrap birthday present" on the appropriate daily to-do list in your planner.

The Family Calendar space is reserved for *time-specific* places you need to go and things you need to do—things like preschool for Karly from 9:00 to 11:20, lunch with Mia and her girls at 11:30, and haircuts for Spencer and Oliver at 4:20. Unless there's a specific time restriction, tasks like "make cookies for the bake sale" should go on your daily to-do list, not your calendar. As moms, our days are fluid and ever-changing; too many restrictions can be frustrating for everyone!

I rarely use the appointment schedules on the daily pages of my planner for just that reason. Writing to-dos in a specific time slot just makes me feel hurried and behind when, inevitably, the time passes and the task isn't done. My exception to this rule is any day that's completely booked with time-sensitive tasks, like the day I'm hosting a big party. If I need to have the potatoes in the oven by 4:30 and the salad made by 5:00, I write those things in the appointment schedule lines.

On a more typical day, I still like to do certain things around the same time of day. I'm not a morning person. I know that I tend to think most clearly in the afternoons, and have more energy for physical work in the evenings. In order to use my time and talents efficiently, I break up my to-do list into three general time chunks. If you think about it, your day is naturally divided into parts. Maybe you think of your day in terms of before work, at work, and after work. Or simply morning, afternoon, and evening.

As the mother of a one-year-old, my life revolves around naptime. There's before nap, when we can go out and about and I can complete tasks that involve my kids. There's naptime (or quiet rest time), when I can accomplish things that require relative quiet and solitude. Then there's after nap (or after school), when my family is bustling with homework and activities and dinner and baths and bedtimes.

Each to-do item falls into one of these time chunks and is placed at the top, in the middle, or at the bottom of my list. (For a visual, check out Appendix C.) Because of this, an item at "the top of the list" may not be nearly as important as an item placed in the middle or at the end. I denote each item's priority in a different way.

Really living your priorities

Organizing your time means deciding what's truly important to you and getting it done. In order to do that, you need to consider the priority of each to-do item. If you don't, you'll end up completing a must-do task at 11:00 at night when you're dog-tired, berating yourself for spending your time on something you could've done tomorrow.

Each morning, or each evening before bed if that's a better time for you, take a few minutes to prayerfully consider your list of tasks for the upcoming day. (Appendix A can help you do your planning.) Write your tasks in the appropriate time chunks, then place a 1, 2, or 3 priority number next to each item. You can use A, B, and C, or another trio—whatever you'd like. When you assign priorities to your tasks, you're focusing on what you really want to do with your time.

If you *have* to get a task done today, mark it a 1. There shouldn't be too many of these—most things could wait until tomorrow if you really think about it. But, if your child is the octopus in tomorrow's school play and her costume still needs six more arms, "sew costume" is definitely a 1.

Your biggest group will be the 2s. These are things you *should* get done today in order to meet your goals and keep your household running smoothly. You're reasonably sure you can accomplish these tasks today, but if you had to put them off until tomorrow, you wouldn't be letting anyone down.

The smallest group is the set of 3s: things you'd love to get done today, but realistically speaking, you probably won't. A checkmark next to a 3 is a happy, unexpected bonus. Don't put too many 3s on your list—they can make your day seem overcrowded and overwhelming, and at the end of the day you'll feel like you didn't get anything done.

Now, I'll admit here that I don't prioritize my tasks *every* day. (Again, my Franklin Planner instructor would be highly disappointed.) Each day I pray over my planner (literally with my hand on it), surrendering the upcoming day to the Lord and asking for His guidance and blessing on my work. Then I take a few minutes to look over my tasks. Most days, I can easily discern what really needs to be done, but if I have a particularly full day with lots of to-dos, I take a few minutes to assign each task a priority number.

This may seem like too much structure for you. Of course, you don't have to do it. You may not need the time chunks because you have an innate sense of what times of day are best for different tasks. Or you may naturally gravitate toward your most important tasks and not need the priority numbers. But if you want to get into the habit of really living your priorities, give this system a try. Separate and prioritize your tasks for a couple of weeks to see whether or not it helps you get the good stuff done.

Throughout your day, refer to your list and work on your first priority items as soon as it's a good time to do so. When you're out of 1s for your time chunk, move on to your 2s, and even 3s if your day is going like clockwork. (It happens sometimes.) When you hit the next part of your day, start with the 1s there.

At the end of the day, after you've been blessed to be able to complete so many of the things on your list, be sure to consider what's left. Obviously, you're not going to bed until all the 1s are checked off, but there may be some 2s and 3s that need to be re-written on future daily lists. And that's OK. You focused on your priorities in the time you had, so you can be satisfied you did your best for your family and for Jesus. You can go to bed with a clear mind and a happy heart.

I'm willing you to read this

If you find you're bumping back the same task again and again, take a good look at it. It's possible it isn't really that pressing, and its related goal needs to be moved on to the Greater To-Do List for another time. It's perfectly fine to do that—remember, you can't do everything at once. You may even decide you don't want to complete that task at all.

It's also possible that you're getting bogged down in things that feel more urgent but are actually less important to you. Again, there are very few things pressing enough to make it into your 1 category, so there should be some room there. If the task is really important to you, bump it up on the priority list and be intentional about making the time to complete it.

If the task is important to you, but you're procrastinating because it's off-putting for some reason, call it a 1 and get it done. Pray about it, then promise yourself a reward for completing it, or get an accountability partner if that's what it takes. Today is your chance to do what's important to you, so do it.

Here's where I can feel some of you thinking, *That's easy for you to say, Miss Organized.* OK, Jesus Moms, I know I'm not much of a procrastinator, but I do understand. I probably have more than my fair share of "willpower," and I still can't count on it.

Willpower fails me when I really, really don't want to do something I should. (Picture me, ready to start cooking a meal that involves handling raw chicken, thinking, *But Travis and the kids love it when we get pizza.*) It fails me when I really, really *do* want to do something I shouldn't. (Picture me at a place called The Chocolate Café, thinking, *Oooo, the Monster Sundae looks awfully good.*)

Actually doing the things that are in line with our goals and priorities can be hard. Usually we need to buckle down and get 'er done. But sometimes, forcing ourselves to do something with a grumpy, weary heart is worse, so we need to give ourselves some grace.

But how can we discern which choice will clear the clutter out of our spirits? Try asking God what His choice is by praying something like this:

Oh Lord, I really do/do not want to do this right now. I'm
feeling weak. I don't know if this is in Your will for me
today, but right now I'm ready to let go.
Please give me a sense of peace about this decision...
or shake me up with Your strength.

I've lifted up this prayer many times. Sometimes, I do feel His peace, the peace that tells me it's perfectly OK not to cook dinner tonight—pizza is *fine*. The peace that allows me to fully enjoy my perfectly *fine* fun-splurge Monster Sundae. The peace that assures me I'm still living life intentionally—I'm intentionally giving myself a break.

But sometimes the Lord shakes me up. He doesn't let me off the hook. I realize in that moment that it *matters* to me that I'm a Jesus Mom living intentionally for my Lord, my family, and myself. I feel—not willpower—but His strength as I start making dinner or order a single scoop of "lite" ice cream.

God knows what's best for you when you're feeling weak. He can lead you toward your goals when the time is right, and

He can give you the ability to take it easy sometimes. Either way, He's leading you toward the still waters of His peace.

Now stop thinking about willpower so you can think about interruptions

As you're happily living your priorities and doing all the things a Jesus Mom should, of course you'll be interrupted. Love those interruptions! Yes, *love* them. Because most likely it'll be a person who's interrupting you: a friend on the phone, someone at the door, or a little person tugging at your sleeve. We can embrace interruptions as opportunities to shine God's love, and besides, interruptions don't always have to stop us from getting things done.

When you're prioritizing, try making little stars next to the tasks you can do without really thinking. All of us have "busy-work" we can do on autopilot. Like when you use ninety-nine percent of your brain power on the conversation you're having with your husband while you use the other one percent to load the dishwasher. (A lot of chores are this way, but again, we're saving those for later.) These are the tasks we can do when we're interrupted by a ringing phone or a chatty family member.

This is not "multitasking" in the sense that you're trying to get lots of things done at once. "Multitasking" is a fake word like "paradigm" or "synergize" or "blurgh"—a strange business myth that really means you do more things poorly at the same time and have to do them again. For example, don't try to complete any less-than-rote task while you're on the phone. That's rude. The person on the other end of the line will be able to tell you're doing it, and you won't be building your relationship with them. (I can hear Travis saying, "No Shan, tell them how you *really* feel.")

If you answer the phone and sense a long conversation coming, glance at the starred items on your list and choose one. While your hands are busy doing something you could do in your sleep, your heart is with the person on the other end of the line. In fact, I find that I'm *more* focused on the conversation because I'm not distracted by the feeling that I should get off the phone and get something done.

These are also great tasks to complete while your kids are playing independently. You can hang around your kids, keep an eye on them, and chat with them about what they're doing while *you're* doing mindless tasks. You're completely available to them if they need your attention or want to engage with you, but you can still get some basic things done. You can also save this kind of busywork to do during a relaxing time when you're watching TV or listening to music.

Most interruptions come from outside sources, but don't forget about the ones that come from your own mind clutter. Little things (and big things) spring to mind, things you want to do or remember. When that happens, try not to get pulled into starting a new task. If possible, write the item down in your planner with its priority number and go back to whatever you were doing.

Sometimes writing a task down will take almost as long as simply completing it. If it's something that will only take a minute or two, go ahead and do it, but as a general rule you're better off finishing what you started. A kind of lethargy sets in when you keep stopping and restarting a task, and soon it feels like you're never going to get that checkmark. Don't let little things distract you and interrupt the flow of your day—unless they're not so little.

When plans go awry (so you had a bad day)

We're the moms, and our days revolve around our families. We love to care for them, so we wouldn't have it any other way. But our reasonably planned days can go right out the window in a heartbeat. Like the moment a child says, "Mom, my ear hurts." Uh-oh, ear infection.

Off we go for a walk-in appointment with the pediatrician, who's always running behind. We wait, and entertain our sick little one, and wait some more…until finally the doctor confirms our mommy diagnosis with one quick peek. Clutching a prescription, we head to the pharmacy, where we sit and wait again. Our poor sweet baby is tired and hungry and cranky because they don't feel so good. And then we realize that *we're* cranky. We just lost four hours of our day, and we don't feel so good, either.

It doesn't always take a mini-catastrophe like a sick kid to turn a great day into a not-so-good one. Even little things can throw us off our stride. Things take longer than we think they should. New things pop up. We run out of something and suddenly we need to run a "quick" errand. Big glasses of milk spill all over papers, and outfits, and floors.

On any given day, a to-do list that looked completely reasonable first thing in the morning can look insurmountable at noon. We get frustrated because we can't do what we want to do. We feel the need to hurry, hurry, hurry. We feel that we don't have the *time* to be the wives and moms and daughters of God we want to be. Talk about your spiritual clutter.

These feelings throw us even more off our stride. Our hearts cry out to the Lord, *What a mess! Why do I even try?* In our discouragement, we start to entertain the common misconception that God doesn't want us to make our own plans. "Man plans, God laughs," right? Wrong. I know it's a Yiddish saying, but it's not even close to Biblical. It's supposedly based upon this verse:

> In his heart a man plans his course,
> But the Lord determines his steps.
>
> *Proverbs 16:9*

Jesus Moms, this is a far, far cry from the Lord laughing at our weak little plans. In fact, it's infinitely comforting. This verse tells us that the Lord will always work His will for us, even if we become misguided. In fact, those delays and unexpected twists may be Him guiding us back on the right path, forcing us to rely on Him for peace and purpose. None of that means He doesn't want us to try to do our best with the time He's given us.

And I'll take it a step further and argue that God *wants* us to take our best shot at prayerfully planning our own course. Consider these verses, straight from His word:

> Commit to the Lord whatever you do,
> and your plans will succeed.
>
> *Proverbs 16:3*

> Do not those who plot evil go astray?
> But those who plan what is good find love and faithfulness.
>
> *Proverbs 14:22*

Even if He has other things in mind for our days (and the weeks and months and years ahead), I believe that the Lord approves of our earnest planning. He loves goals that involve serving Him, building our relationships, and enjoying our life here on Earth. He wants us to fill our days with purpose as we live our days for Him— even when things don't go our way.

My husband's favorite nickname for me is "Shan with a Plan." That's because I usually have one. And I don't love it when my plan is disrupted, which is, let's face it, a lot of the time. I have a husband who doesn't really like having a plan, and three kids who never seem to have one. My day rarely goes the way I envisioned it at 6:30 in the morning. I plan and organize and prepare, then I have to do my best to go with the flow when life happens.

When my plans go awry it helps me to stop, take a deep breath, and get realistic. I take a moment to thank God that this crazy day is "only a speed bump in the great road of life" (a phrase I inherited from my parents—it's a classic in my family). Sometimes, I even calm my heart by singing to Him, which, not coincidentally, requires deep, even breathing.

When I was twelve years old, I learned a little praise song based on this well-known verse:

Cast all your anxiety on Him because He cares for you.

I Peter 5:7

I remember singing that little song on my way to take my college entrance exams. I prayed over I Peter 5:7 on my first day of student teaching. And, of course, I leaned heavily on this verse as I struggled with clinical anxiety. The Lord certainly knew the plans He had for me when He wrote those words on the tablet of my heart. I know I can cast my cares upon Him and be filled with grace and peace.

Jesus Moms, these kinds of days happen to us all and we can always find comfort in the Lord. Remember that Christ is on the throne and that He has it all under control. Remember that His ways are higher than your ways and His thoughts are higher than your thoughts, and look for His will in what's happening. Try meditating on a favorite praise song or Bible verse to bring you through a stressful moment and into a spirit of peace. Count some of the blessings He's given you, especially the ones related to whatever has tripped you up. And remember that you're a very, very beloved daughter of God.

After your heart is calm and your spirit is lifted up, you'll need to take a moment to re-plan your day. Focus on getting the 1s done, no matter what time of day you were originally planning on doing them. With a little bit of erasing, you can change most of the priority 2 tasks into priority 3s, or move them to a different day altogether. You may also need to add new tasks, including phone calls or e-mails to cancel and reschedule plans.

You can do these things with the peace of mind that comes from knowing that yes, you are organized, and yes, you are managing your time. You have a big-picture plan, and the important things in your life *will* get done. On a frustrating day, or indeed on any given day, you can rest in the fact that you're doing your best for God and your family. You're not buried under a pile of overwhelming tasks—you're using them like bricks to build your home for your family, with Jesus as your Perfect Cornerstone.

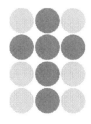

Chapter 4

Chores

OK, get ready for an amazingly exciting topic: Chores!

No, really, I love this part. It *is* exciting to make a chore plan. We moms spend so much of our time doing chores that we might as well do them efficiently and with a happy heart. Organizing our chores is a great way to save time and unnecessary effort…and reduce our spiritual clutter.

Most moms think about chores way too much. *The laundry is really piling up. I'll throw in a load right after I…*and then you're off and running, on to something else. An hour later it zings you again—*I have got to throw that laundry in! We're running out of underwear.* And then the phone rings. And so on. And at the end of the day, you still have no underwear for tomorrow. Or it's clean, but it's piled up on the bed you'd really like to get in.

Jesus Moms, the Lord doesn't want you to live this way, so far from His peace! You can choose to exterminate the chore-related thoughts that are buzzing around your mind, stinging your heart. By giving thought to your ways, you'll prayerfully discover a chore plan that will help you to feel on top of things. You'll know that life is happening and *you're getting it done.*

When you have that kind of chore system, you can be thankful to the Lord and enjoy each task. You can intentionally clear out some of your chore-related spiritual clutter with a purposeful attitude of gratitude. Instead of thinking, *I have to do this,* you can decide, *I get to do this.*

Thinking with a get-to attitude makes every chore better, even dealing with raw chicken, the Grand Epitome of Things I Hate to Do. Instead of thinking, *I have to cut up this raw chicken, gross, Gross, GROSS. I hate cooking and I don't even like chicken,* I decide to think, *I get to cut up this chicken and provide a meal for my family. I get to cut up this chicken for a recipe my husband enjoys. Thank you, Lord.* Seriously, it's such a blessing to be able to think this way, and a great chore plan can really help.

Mopping for Jesus

As Jesus Moms, we *get* to do chores. We want to keep our

homes running smoothly. We deeply desire to be good stewards of the Lord's tremendous blessings by completing our household chores. And we want to do it all with a happy, uncluttered spirit! The Apostle Paul said:

> Whatever you do, work at it with all your heart, as working for the Lord, not for men, since you know that you will receive an inheritance from the Lord as a reward.
> It is the Lord Jesus Christ you are serving.
>
> *Colossians 3:23 & 24*

Now, when you look at this scripture in context, you'll notice that Paul wasn't talking to the preachers or the missionaries or the teachers of The Word whose work was so obviously meaningful. No, when he wrote those words he was specifically addressing the slaves of Colossae, the ones who were cooking and cleaning and washing the clothes. Even our most insignificant household chores are work we can—and should—do for the Lord. Jesus Moms, we don't want to mope about our chores, we want to mop for Jesus!

With an organized chore plan, you'll be able to relax about your chores and do them in the peaceful presence of the Lord. In this chapter and the next, we're going to clean that chore clutter out of your spirit. We're going to focus on the chores you do on a daily and weekly basis, the things that can bug you all the time because it feels like they're never, ever actually done. Or if you do get them finished, you turn around and it's time to start again.

The key to doing these chores is to do them as little as possible. Do I hear an "Amen," Jesus Moms? This statement isn't as obvious as it sounds. Because some chores feel like they need to be done all the time, we can over do it. We do them too often, or in a completely inefficient, helter-skelter way.

So ask yourself, what chores do you *want* to do, and how often do you *need* to do them? What is the least amount of chore work that will still satisfy your heart and make you feel like a great mom, wife, and daughter of God?

God doesn't give us bonus points for having the cleanest house in the neighborhood, or for having our laundry done each night. Supermom perfectionism isn't the goal of chore organization. You're getting organized so you can spend *less* time on your chores and *more* time with your family.

In college, I used to hear fellow students using the phrase "C+ works." At my university, if you earned a "C+" in a course, then you passed it. While I was earnestly burning the midnight oil to get the best grade in the class, other kids were saying "C+ works" and going to bed. They realized they didn't need "As" to get their hands on a college diploma that looked exactly like mine. As I've mellowed with age, I've adopted this phrase as well—because I still need it. (True nerdiness never dies.) Especially when it comes to housework, "C+" really does work.

Your comfort with structure, or the lack of it

Now, I fully realize there are moms out there who don't care if they have the cleanest house on the block, moms who *invented* "C+ works." Perhaps the idea of should-do cleaning thoughts cluttering up your spirit just doesn't strike a chord in your heart. If you're one of those moms, then you are very, very blessed. You're right in the middle of a Jesus Mom Organizational Continuum, where different moms embrace different amounts of structure, and all of them are loving and serving the Lord.

On one end, we have the moms who love structure. If you're a Type-A mom, your house is ship-shape, and when you decide something needs to be done, you do it. Your husband may ask, "Honey, what did you do all day?"—because you make it look too easy! But inside, your spirit is cluttered. You worry that you're missing something...that things aren't *perfect*. You feel like you can't get a break because things *always* need to be done. You're reading this book in order to glean a hint or two about how to run your home even more efficiently. I think I can help you out there, and get you to relax a bit, too.

On the other hand, it's possible you're a mom who's a little *too* laid back (but still a great one!). Maybe this strikes more of a chord: Things in your house don't get done. You're late for appointments and your kid's permission slips go unsigned. Your husband also asks, "Soooo, what did you do all day?"—but it's his not-so-subtle hint that the house is a mess. Even if things aren't *that* bad, you may feel things slipping out of your control. Your house isn't as clean or organized as you would like it to be. In your innermost heart, you know you need to step it up a notch, and that's why you're reading this book. If that's you, read on, Sister.

If you're somewhere in the middle when it comes to structured organization, take a moment to thank the Lord. You don't feel undue pressure to get chores done. Your house is in fine shape because you do your chores as they come up. You still have spiritual clutter to clear out, but it might not be about chores. If you don't feel the need for a chore schedule—or even worse, if it would stress you out—then you shouldn't have one. Don't fix what's not broken.

Occasionally, I go bowling with family or friends, and I've discovered that I'm a bad bowler. Pitiful, actually. But the thing is, I don't really care. I don't have a burning desire to be a better bowler. For me, bowling is about having fun with people I love, and wearing weird but somehow cute shoes, and eating pizza, and feeling absolutely delighted when I fling my ball down the lane and it actually knocks down a pin or two.

The only time I *don't* have fun at the bowling alley is when I go with someone who feels compelled to teach me how to improve my bowling skills. This well-meant instruction makes me tense. Suddenly I feel pressure to "succeed" at bowling, and my spirit gets cluttered with "how-tos" and "shoulds" and other people's expectations. I have to stop and remind myself that I don't actually value bowling prowess. Then I can tell my helper that, although I appreciate his or her efforts, I just want to relax and enjoy the night.

I want to be *your* helper as you organize your household, but I also want you to relax and enjoy your life. I'll never ask you to get organized for the sake of being organized. You can't get rid of your spiritual clutter by holding yourself to someone else's standards—in fact, you'll only make it worse.

I truly feel that every mom needs a planner. We're in charge of too much *not* to have a way to keep it all together. Even less-structured moms will benefit greatly from writing down goals, hanging up a Family Calendar, and using a planner in a very basic way to stay organized. Beyond that, only you and Jesus know what "should-do" thoughts are cluttering up your spirit.

You may not have a lot of spiritual clutter about chores, and if so, I don't want to give you any! Keep reading for ideas about chore management that appeal to you, but feel free to pick and choose the things that will work for you and your family. However, as you're giving thought to your ways you may realize that you *do* have bothersome chore thoughts swirling around in your head, keeping you from enjoying your home, that wonderful blessing from God. That's when you should consider making chore cards.

Chore cards (and the happy sound they make)

It's time to go back to your Goal List to look for any chore-related goals, and to consider all of the other chores you want to get done. Let's get those persistent *I've gotta do that* thoughts about chores out of your head by writing them down. Then you can let them go, reducing your spiritual clutter and calming your heart.

When tackling your personal and project-oriented goals, you wrote to-dos on your daily planner pages. The chores we've been talking about—like cleaning, laundry, and errands—are too repetitive for that. It's a waste of time to write them in your planner, day after day and week after week. I know, because I used to do it. Yuck. Until I discovered chore cards.

Chore cards are easy and inexpensive to make. Essentially, you write your chores on index cards. (Yes, actual index cards. Bear with me.) I cut each card into four long strips and write my chores on those. When I first tried this system, I neatly wrote all of my chores on 3x5 index cards—they were beautiful. Then I actually tried to use them, and found that one day's worth of chores covered most of my kitchen counter. It was completely overwhelming! With the cards cut into strips, you can lay a whole day's worth of chores in one neat column, right alongside your planner and Family Calendar, like a second to-do list. (For a visual, check out Appendix C.)

You'll also need an index card file box to hold them, with dividers for seven sections: Daily, Monday, Tuesday, Wednesday, Thursday, Friday, and Monthly. (Monthly chores are coming up in Chapter 6.) My box didn't come with dividers, so I made my own by putting self-adhesive tabs on seven index cards. If you're a working mom, or if your family has an untraditional schedule, you may want to make an additional section for Saturday.

White index card strips are great for your daily tasks, but it's nice to buy colored index cards for the weekday sections (Monday-Friday). They usually come in packs with five colors, so you can easily assign a different color to each weekday. I recommend this, not only because I'm the kind of girl who enjoys color coding things, but because it's easier on our brains to replace the cards by matching the colors. Also, if a card makes its way into the wrong section by accident, you'll notice it right away.

Each time you finish a chore, you place its chore card back in the box until the next day, or week, or even month. The little clicking sound the cards make when you toss them back in the box is just as satisfying as a checkmark on your to-do list. That sound makes me happy: click, click, click! (What did I say about true nerdiness? Watch out, Jesus Moms—there's more!)

Yes, I'm a bit of a dinosaur

Chore cards are found in a lot of classic organizing books (although I'll be giving you my own Jesus Mom version). This isn't a new idea, it's an old one, dating back to before the advent of super duper laptop computers, smart phones, tablets, and other technologies that have the potential to aggravate you just as much as not being organized at all. Ah, technology.

You may have noticed that I didn't spend any time talking about technology-based planner systems and calendars and all of that good stuff. I am a traditional girl. I like being able to access my plan for the day without it dying because the battery needs to be charged, or erasing because I forgot to hit save. I'm actually typing on a typewriter right now. (Not really.)

I do love my chore cards. I've had the same box for ten years. It's right next to my paper-based daily planner. Jesus Moms, computers crash, smart phones get lost, and software changes, but *office supplies are forever.*

Seriously, I like the flexibility of actual chore cards. Using them makes it easier to swap chore days when it's a good idea to do so. If you're hosting a special social event for your moms' group on Wednesday, you can move your cleaning chores to Tuesday and split your usual Wednesday chores between Thursday and Friday. Or if you've just had a crazy day, you can bump your chores back to the next day by placing them in with tomorrow's cards.

Even more, I like keeping my paper-based planner and chore cards far away from the temptations of electronic media. I like being able to glance at my to-do list and chore card line-up without the enticement to hop online or check my e-mail (again) or see how many likes Organizing *You* Ministries has on Facebook (again) or read my friends' blogs. (*Oooo, she has a new post! It's about procrastinating.*)

Online social media can work like a magnetic force, pulling our minds away from our current tasks—our current *lives*—and into cyberspace. Keeping your time and chore management systems off-line may help you to manage your time in a different way: you'll have more of it when you keep yourself in the real world, doing what's really important to you and furthering God's Kingdom here on Earth.

Now, even after those totally logical and even heartstring-tugging points, some of you are still thinking, *Come on, Shannon, there's got to be an app for that.* OK, Technology Girls, go ahead and check out the fancy electronic systems. (Sadly, I can't tell you about the different electronic options, because by the time you read this the technology will be new and different anyway.) Truly, you may find something that works really well for you.

But please, do me a favor and read about the chore cards

regardless, because then you'll be better able to discern what you want your technology to do for you…and maybe you'll end up back in the paper days with me! (You never know.)

Making chores a priority

Chore cards work together with your planner to keep you living your priorities. As you prayerfully prepare for the upcoming day, arrange the daily and day-of-the-week cards you need in a column next to your planner, in time chunks just like your to-dos. Then, throughout the day, glance over your to-do list and chore cards to decide what you'd like to do next. Easy, right? But where do the chore cards fall in your 1, 2, or 3 task priority assignments?

Daily and weekly chores are almost always priority 2 items. They're things we'd like to do to keep our households running smoothly, but if they don't happen today, the world won't end. When choosing a task from my daily planner list and chore card line-up, I try to complete my chores *after* the 1 tasks in my time chunk, but *before* the 2s. Rolling chores back can make for an overwhelming tomorrow, so it's often better to postpone the 2 and 3 priority items written on your daily to-do list.

Jesus Moms, I love my chore cards. I lay them out every day. With this system, I never worry that the laundry is piling up, or that I really should vacuum, or that things are slipping away from me in general. Those cards help me clear out my spiritual clutter and enjoy taking care of my family, because I know I'm doing what I want to do just as much as I need to do it. God and I made a chore plan together and I just love it—and I think you will, too! So let's start on *your* pretty colored cards.

What to write on those beautifully color-coded cards

Well, actually, let's start with the white daily ones. You won't have to write down many daily chores because they don't usually clutter up your spirit—you do most of them without thinking. For example, you rarely have to remind yourself to load the dishwasher. Thoughts about loading the dishwasher don't clutter up your brain, making you feel frazzled and stressed. You just do it.

Or maybe you don't.

Loading the dishwasher may be for you what taking out the trash is for me—a chore that makes us say "ugh." Left to my own devices, I tend to procrastinate, secretly hoping my husband will take it out (which he sometimes does). Or I forget about the trash until it becomes a great, overflowing mound (gross). That's why I actually have "take out the trash" on one of my white daily chore cards.

Chances are, you won't. Chore cards are very individual things, especially the daily ones. Daily chore cards should cover all of the daily things that you *forget* or *dislike*.

Sometimes you really just forget things, even if they're important. If you have a chore card telling you to feed the cat, you'll be much more likely to remember to do it. Your cat will thank you (or at least stop destroying your belongings in protest).

You'll benefit from making chore cards for disliked daily tasks as well. When you place the chore card into one of your three time chunk groups, you're forced to choose the approximate time of day that's best to complete it, hopefully making it easier and avoiding procrastination. And trust me, when you've completed an especially yucky chore, you'll really chuck that card back into the box—CLICK! It's a small but satisfying thing that makes you feel better about doing chores you don't like.

Only you know what daily tasks you forget or dislike. You may want to write daily cards to remind you to take your medications, exercise, pack school lunches, prepare dinner, write in a journal, or have a prayer or devotional time. (I have a longer list of daily chore card ideas for you in Appendix D—but only make a card if you really need the reminder. The fewer daily cards you have, the better.)

Now, notice that those aren't all technically "chores," especially that last one. Don't feel badly about putting your prayer or devotional time on a chore card—it's incredibly helpful. You'll lay that card by your planner each day, and let me tell you, it stings to put it back in the box, undone, at the end of the day. Writing "Time with Jesus" on a card isn't making it a chore, Jesus Moms, it's making it a *priority*.

Your chore cards can have anything on them. If you want to do something every day with intention, put it on a white daily chore card. This is a great time to think about some of the actual clutter in your house. You should think about the minimum amount of "straightening up" you want to do each day in order to keep your family members comfortable (i.e., not tripping over things).

Some of your family members might not even see that day-to-day clutter, but one or two of them may be bothered by out-of-place stuff. As a Jesus Mom, you want your whole family to be at ease in your home, so you should discern which family member is the *most* disturbed by mess. (That may be you. In my house, it's definitely me.) Try to be considerate of their (your) feelings and help them (yourself) relax by doing some basic straightening up once or twice a day.

Even if no one living in your house minds a little mess, you should still pick up occasionally so the clutter doesn't get out of hand, and so an I-was-just-in-the-neighborhood guest doesn't stress you out. You know the feeling: your friend pops by and you can't believe you're letting her see your house like this! Now, if you're a Type-A gal, keep in mind that a certain amount of mess makes a house feel homey and lived-in. However, if you stand in the doorway using your body as a shield so your visitor can't see into your home, you may want to give some thought to your ways.

If you have spiritual clutter about physical clutter, then write a daily chore card that encourages you to walk through your house for a quick pick-up. You could straighten up first thing in the morning, after lunch, or before you go to bed—whenever is best for you. If you want to do it more than once, then write two daily chore cards and lay them out in the appropriate time chunks.

And don't forget about your Goal List! Now's the time to review your chore-related goals, and even the personal and project-oriented ones, to find things you'd like to remember to do every day. Write them on your white daily chore cards, or do it your own way, possibly by posting a typed list on your fridge or keeping a checklist on your smart phone. No matter how you decide to keep track of them, choose daily tasks that will help you reach your goals and be the mom and woman of God you want to be.

The Big Five

Next are the days-of-the-week cards, the pretty colored ones you've chosen for Monday, Tuesday, Wednesday, Thursday, and Friday. Moms usually have the best chance of getting their chores done on weekdays, the five days of the week with the greatest semblance of order and routine. But what do we do, and when?

Lots of mommy chores can be grouped into what I call "The Big Five": Cleaning, Laundry, Errands, Communicating, and Projects. Wait, did you think "The Big Five" was supposed to refer to the five weekdays? No, I meant the chores—but since there are five of each, why not put them together?

Many moms refer to their days in terms of their chores, with phrases like "today's Cleaning Day" or "tomorrow's my Laundry Day." It doesn't sound like fun to name your days after chores, but lots of moms do this because it works.

The *time* benefit is that you'll do your chores much more efficiently when you group like chores together. As long as you've got a grip on your cleaning caddy and have yourself in an I-*get*-to-clean-potties frame of mind, you might as well clean all of your bathrooms. Run all of your errands while you're already out. Keep those loads of laundry moving right along.

But there's also a *heart* benefit to grouping your chores. Once you've completed a big chore, you don't have to worry about that chore for *the next six days*. Sure, there's always cleaning to be done, but it's a relief to know that you don't have to do it today. You can let it go completely because you know you'll get to it on Cleaning Day.

And as a bonus, this kind of system grants you a sense of satisfaction and accomplishment that's often missing in mommy living—the feeling that the chore is *done*. At the end of Laundry Day, *The Laundry is Done*! For a whole week! Aren't you excited for that feeling? (See, I told you chore planning was fun.)

But first, take some time to pray over what you've read about so far. Talk with God about your chore attitude and about daily chores you'd like to do for your family and for Him. Then, get your heart ready to tackle The Big Five weekly chores.

Chapter 5

The Big Five

Let's dive into your weekday chores so you can clear out that spiritual clutter and do your chores with joy for Jesus!

Cleaning Day

Once a week, your house most likely needs a good clean. A scrub-the-potties, wipe-out-the-microwave, vacuum-the-whole-place kind of clean. I like to make Friday my Cleaning Day because we usually have company on the weekends. If you host a Tuesday night Bible study in your home, then by all means clean on Monday or Tuesday. Pick the day that works best for you and your family. (Working Moms, for you it might be Saturday—I'll have more thoughts for you in a bit.)

Your house requires its own individual kind and amount of cleaning. Take a tour of your house to decide what a once-a-week cleaning should involve for you. Some chores you may want to write on weekly cards include dusting, spot cleaning kitchen cabinets and backsplashes, wiping down kitchen appliances, cleaning mirrors and glass surfaces, sweeping, cleaning bathrooms, mopping, and vacuuming.

Remember, you're writing down the cleaning chores you *want* to do, and then deciding exactly how infrequently you *need* to do them in order to satisfy your heart. There are plenty of cleaning chores that don't need to be done once a week. If dusting once a week feels necessary in your house, then do it. But if your dust rag is way too clean at the end of a sincere dusting effort, try dusting every other week and see how that feels.

After you've chosen your weekly Cleaning Day, you may also want to make a "pick up the house" chore card for the night *before* Cleaning Day. Recruit your husband and kids to spend a little time each Cleaning Day Eve helping you ready your house for a good clean.[1] They don't have to pick up *everything* (trust me, I've swept around more Lego cities, princess doll tea parties, and

---

1 For a fun way to encourage your kid(s) to help with household chores, check out the "Chore Passports For Kids" article on OrganizingJesusMoms.com.

piles of paperwork than I can count), but your family can work together to complete the "cleaning" you have to do before you can actually clean! On Cleaning Day itself, you'll make quick work of your chores…and sweep the *This place is a mess!* thoughts right out of your spirit.

Laundry Day

I will confess, I love Laundry Day.

Bright and early on Thursday mornings, I line up my laundry baskets in the hallway outside the laundry room and start the first load. Karly, Oliver, and I generally stay in our pajamas until at least noon (all of our clothes are in the wash anyway, right?). I play with the kids between loads, and let them choose a TV show for us to watch while I'm folding the warm, clean clothes. It's a wonderful, laid back, lazy day.

Hopefully you'll be able to make Laundry Day a "relaxing" day around your house, too. Choose the day of the week with the fewest outside commitments, and try not to schedule appointments or playdates that day of the week. Your kids will love it, and you'll enjoy how your husband and kids adjust to the laundry schedule. Your sweethearts will stop asking you to wash their favorite outfits *right now*—they'll know they have to wait until Laundry Day!

Admittedly, you do have to be diligent to finish all your laundry in a day. If possible, keep the loads moving right along and avoid wrinkles by folding the laundry as soon as you take it out of the dryer. You can put it away as you go, or wait until a time of day that's better for you. I usually wait until the late afternoon—when all of the laundry is clean and folded, putting the clothes away is quick work.

Of course, spills and dirt and other stains happen, so I do throw in the occasional load of laundry on the other six days of the week. When I do, I make sure to write "one load of laundry" on my daily to-do list so I don't forget the wet clothes in the washer. Having the to-do in my planner also gives me the chance to make a happy checkmark (uh-*huh*!) after the load of laundry is clean and put away.

In terms of chore cards, laundry is pretty straightforward. I have one "Laundry" chore card that covers all of my family's clothing and towels. If your standards are higher than mine, you may want to write an "Ironing" chore card—it is easier to do when the clothes are freshly washed.

It's even easier when your husband does it out of pity. I can't iron. Luckily, being a fantastic laundress is about as important to me as being a great bowler. I just don't have a lot of spiritual clutter about laundry, as may be evidenced by this fact: I have one more Laundry Day chore card that reads "wash bedding." This card has a star on it to denote that it's an every-other-week chore.

Now, I know some of you are thinking, *She doesn't wash her sheets every week? That's disgusting!* But, I also guarantee that others of you are thinking, *She washes her sheets every other week? I only wash mine once a month. Or so. When* was *the last time I washed my sheets?* Jesus Moms, looking in another mom's chore box would be like reading her diary! Do your chores only as frequently as *you* need to in order to keep your spirit free of clutter.

Errand Day

Busy moms can run errands too often and in an inefficient, haphazard way (is this ringing any bells, Jesus Moms?). When you group errands together on an Errand Day, you can save time, gasoline, and maybe even a little spending money. After all, you'll make fewer impulsive purchases if you're not in stores as often. And, if you wait until Errand Day to purchase nonessentials, you may decide you don't really need them after all.

Best of all, you'll only have to get yourself and any kids coming along for the ride out of the house, with shopping lists and coupons in tow, once a week—sometimes that feels like half the battle! At the Upton house, Tuesdays are the days we're out and about, running errands. We go out in the morning and try to make it home by lunchtime, or we meet friends for lunch since we're already out of the house.

If you're running multiple errands with your kids, you can prepare for the car ride with books and other activities. You can also mentally prepare your kids for a longer trip, instead of promising them a quick trip out to get shoes, but then deciding to stop at the dry cleaner's, and then remembering that you're out of milk. Kids don't love that. Moms don't either.

Of course there will be exceptions to the rule, but with planning, most errands really can wait until Errand Day. You'll want to plan meals ahead so you only have to shop for groceries once a week (we'll talk more about meal planning in Chapter 8). You'll also need to stock your home with extra essentials like toilet paper so you can avoid emergency trips to the store (now *those* clutter my spirit!).

Errand Day doesn't require chore cards, just shopping lists and a plan. Before you leave, take the time to attach your coupons to the shopping lists for each store. Take a look at all of the errands you need to run and decide upon the most efficient route for you. If you need groceries, you should probably get those last so the chocolate doesn't melt in your car.

You should also set aside some Errand Day time to deal with the results of your errands. I allot some of my afternoon time chunk for this. If I bought a frame, I put the picture in it. If I bought a gift, I wrap it. You can use that time to file receipts, cut up vegetables, open boxes, remove tags, and get out the wire cutters if you happened to buy anything from Fisher Price.

The number of errands on your list will vary week by week. Sometimes you won't have many errands to run (bonus!), and sometimes you may have to go back out in the evening in order to finish your errands. Either way, at the end of the day, you'll have everything you need to keep your family humming along for another week. Then you can give yourself—and your credit card—a breather!

Communication Day

Every mom could use a Communication Day—a day when you can catch up on your e-mails and pay bills and address birthday cards and write thank-you notes and call your grandma. God made women to communicate! Our efforts to communicate with our loved ones and friends are fantastic because, through them, we're strengthening our relationships.

Unfortunately, we often put these tasks on the back burner, pushing them aside in favor of things that seem more urgent. And every mom knows that sidling up to a computer or quietly dialing a phone will rouse even the most contentedly playing child into a state of immediate need! At the end of the day, nothing clouds our Jesus Mom spirits more than the feeling that we failed to care for someone—failed to reach out to someone by showing our interest or our thanks or our love.

You can complete these kinds of chores more efficiently and with a happier spirit if you decide to set a Communication Day. In order to communicate your love effectively, especially in writing, try setting aside a time of quiet concentration to focus your heart on these tasks, maybe early in the morning or late at night. If your kids are in school or still napping, or if you have a quiet break time at work, then you already have some quiet time built into the middle of your day.

If your kids are with you all day, it's OK—and maybe even good for them—to tell them that they need to entertain themselves for a while. First, spend some fun time focused solely on them, then tell them that you need some quiet time to concentrate. Try to give them an idea of how long it will be and stick to it—even if Pinterest is calling!

Online time will probably be a big part of your Communication Day because different technologies offer great ways to stay connected with your family and friends. That's a good thing, unless being connected to the Internet is making you less connected to your husband and kids. We all know people who spend mass quantities of time on social networking websites, or are absorbed in other technologies.

You know how no one ever says, "I wish I'd spent more time

working" on their death bed? Well, no one's ever going to say, "I wish I'd spent more time on Facebook," either. Jesus Moms, if your spirit is cluttered with too-much-time-online guilt, consider making Communication Day the *only* day you allow yourself to communicate in this way. Tell your friends, "I'm only checking this on Mondays now—if you want to get in touch with me sooner, just give me a call!" or "just text me!" or whatever you'd like. Everyone will live. I know this sounds harsh, but it's an easy way to keep yourself accountable.

At the very least, consistently allocate one short quiet time each day to respond to e-mails and take care of your other electronic communications. You could even put this on a daily chore card, so when you put it back in the box, you'll know you're offline for the rest of the day. You can intentionally make the choice to be present with your kids, your husband, and the Lord.

Many of the tasks you complete on Communication Day will be required responses. Returning phone calls and replying to e-mails. Dealing with any actual mail that's piled up on you, including bills. Writing thank-you notes. Filling out and returning school forms and other paperwork. But *you* can initiate some of the communication, too. Communication Day is the perfect time to work towards the relationship goals on your Goal List.

It may feel a little cheesy, but you can use chore cards to strengthen your relationships with your husband, kids, and other loved ones. Be creative, and remember to give them the kind of love that they most enjoy receiving. For example, I have a chore card which prompts me to shower my hubby with a little extra love each Communication Day.

Travis appreciates affirming words, so I try to write a little love note for him once a week and leave it where he's sure to find it. Sometimes I'll send him an e-mail or leave him a voice message at work instead, or shake it up by giving him a little gift or completing one of his chores. I've been doing this for years and he still hasn't figured out that I do it like clockwork every Monday.

I like to make Monday my Communication Day so I can take care of the things that slid a bit over the weekend and get a fresh start to the week. It's also a great day to take those baby steps toward my personal and project-oriented goals. It's a lighter chore day, so I often write those specific, goal-driven tasks in my daily planner on Mondays.

In fact, many of the things you need to do on Communication Day will be things you've written in your planner. If you find yourself thinking of a stressed-out friend and feel a nudge to write her a note, write that task down on the daily to-do list for your next Communication Day. If someone gives you a gift or does anything else to make you feel grateful, jot down a reminder to write a thank-you note then, too.

Instead of trying to squeeze in a quick note between loads of laundry, you'll be able to prayerfully prepare for your designated quiet time. You'll complete your communication tasks more quickly, and with a better spirit. Your heart will be in a Christ-centered attitude of caring and love that the people in your life will be able to feel.

Project Day

Project Day, also known as You Day, is the best day of the week. This is the day to set aside some time, hopefully most of your best time chunk, to work on things that aren't so repetitive. Specifically, you'll be completing projects (this is when you get to clean out that closet!) and indulging in hobbies.

Did I say indulge? In the big chore chapter? Yes, I did. Jesus Moms, we all know that we're better wives, moms, and daughters of God when we take the time to do the things we want to do. I won't go into a big diatribe; you've heard it all before. If one more person tells you that taking some "Me Time" is like putting the airplane emergency air mask on yourself first, you'll probably hit them. But, you know it's true—*you need to schedule some time for things that fill you up and give you joy in the Lord.*

OK, I feel pretty strongly about this, so I guess I'll allow myself a teeny, tiny diatribe: Have you ever been at a moms group meeting where the icebreaker question is, "What do you like to do with your free time?" If you have, then you know there will be at least one mom who'll sigh and say, "What's free time? I don't have any free time." Sometimes moms say this because they feel the competitive urge to demonstrate that they have it harder than you do, even though they know motherhood isn't a competition. Sometimes they feel the need to prove their worth, even when they know in their hearts that their true worth is in Jesus. And sometimes they just want someone to commiserate with them, because they know we've all felt the same way at one time or another!

However, the existence of a woman with no free time is a mommy myth. Even wonderful, well-meaning moms find themselves thinking they don't have any free time—but they do. Do they watch TV with their husbands at night after their kids go to bed? Do they have Facebook accounts? Do they meet up with friends to exercise or shop? Are they sitting at that *moms group meeting* saying they don't have any free time?

We've all had those poor-me thoughts: *I never get any time to myself. I never get to do anything fun. I never get to read any more, or scrapbook, or just take a nap.* No matter how selfless you are, thoughts like these can cloud your spirit. They rob you of your sense of peace and make you cranky with your family. You feel put-upon and ungrateful, and those feelings distance you from the Lord. You can clear this kind of clutter right out of your spirit by embracing your free time.

Every mom has free time. You just have to recognize how you spend it, and decide to allow that time to refresh your spirit. If you're going to spend some fun time online, don't just stumble into it. Schedule time, make yourself some coffee or tea, and decide to view that time as the treat it is. If you watch TV to unwind at night, do some deep breathing and allow your body to really relax instead of fidgeting and feeling like you should be doing something else. View your time to exercise or shop or participate in a moms group, not as time that you *have* to take, but as time you choose to spend feeling uplifted and spiritually filled.

Now I'm going to ask you to take it one step further and challenge you to really contemplate those "relaxing" things—are those pursuits *really* how you want to spend your free time? Do you really want to be on the computer so much, or watching so much TV? Do you spend too much time shopping or texting friends? Are you really enjoying your moms group time? You may need to downsize some of these activities so you can spend your free time doing the things you really love. Be a force against the "busy" in your life, and let your kids see that you can relax.

Jesus Moms, as you do this, and begin to use your new time and chore management tools, you'll be able to find a few hours a week to work on projects or enjoy your hobbies. After you've chosen a weekly Project Day, avoid assigning any other weekly chores to that day. Also, try not to write independent tasks on your

Project Day's daily to-do list.

Project Day can be the best day of a Jesus Mom's week—a day to anticipate. Instead of thinking, *I'll never get to that project,* or, *I never get to relax,* I think, *I'll be working on that project before I know it,* or, *I'll get to relax and do some knitting in just a few days!* Sometimes I'll choose the music I want to listen to, or a special snack I want to enjoy (chocolate), days in advance. It's amazing how just thinking about a You Day can refresh your spirit!

When you get to Project Day, fill your heart with happiness by taking the time to work on something that's important to you. Attack that messy guest room, or get those photos off your digital camera, or try that amazing four-hour recipe and have a gourmet dinner. You'll get a distinct sense of accomplishment, because unlike your chores, you won't have to do the project over again next week. You did it! A goal has been completed! Happy checkmark, uh-*huh*!

Indulging (there's that word again) in your hobbies is another great way to clear your spiritual clutter. What gives you joy in the Lord? If you're like my crazy neighbor Debi and you actually enjoy running, then run like the wind. You may want to relax by reading intellectually stimulating books (like this one!), or those magazines that have been piling up. Pop in that movie you've been wanting to see and knit away… Yes, *in the middle of the day.*

I love to scrapbook on my You Day, and if I can squeeze some in on Sunday afternoons, I do that, too. God didn't make it a day of rest for nothing!

Those random weekly chores

Of course, many chores don't fall into one of these five categories—those chores that can slip under our radar. We seldom forget we need to clean, but we may forget to water the plants until they're almost dead. You probably have lots of once-a-week chores that are perfect for chore cards.

Once a week, you can scan your refrigerator and pantry for old food to toss. Take your trash and recycling out to the curb (a good thing to do the day after you toss the old food). Water those indoor plants and weed your flower beds. Complete your weekly Bible study homework or just spend some extra time in the Word. Take a few photos or a little video of your kids. Plan a fun family night once a week, making your goal of a closer family into a reality.

These are just suggestions, and Appendix D has even more. The point is for you to think about your chores and review your Goal List to find those random, repetitive things *you* want to put on a weekly chore card. If there's something you'd like to do twice a week, write it on two cards. For every-other-week tasks, put a little star on the chore card so you know you don't need to lay it out every week.

Since you'll do these random chores on weekdays, you should write them on the colored index card strips. But don't write them all on blue ones just because it's your favorite color (you know you want to). Hold on! You need to assess which of your weekdays will be lighter chore days, like Communication Day or Errand Day, and assign these extra tasks there. Just don't put anything extra on Project Day…and don't make chore cards for Sundays at all.

Working for the weekend

Speaking of Sundays, what about the weekends? Without a good chore plan, you may spend the weekend running around, trying to "catch up" before another week begins. But if you've organized your chores and to-dos into a solid weekday plan, you'll be able to relax and enjoy being with your family on Saturdays and Sundays.

Each Saturday and Sunday morning, I do lay out my daily chore cards, but I try to be more relaxed about what I want to get done. Some of those cards go right back in the box (click, click, click!). Sometimes we'll do project-oriented chores, especially outdoor ones, together as a family. There are also plenty of tasks

I need to write down in my planner to keep up with our busy weekends.

Upton family weekends are usually hoppin' with special outings and social events. We're blessed to have lots of family and friends nearby, and my husband is a very social guy. But, as my friend Aimee says, if my husband is the gas in our family, then I'm the brakes. If I feel we're getting over-scheduled, I'll block out a weekend just for hanging around. And each week we intentionally observe Sunday as a day of rest.

Even Jesus Moms can lose sight of the Sabbath and treat Sunday as a second Saturday. It's not. God set the Sabbath apart for Himself and for us. He wants us to bring ourselves to Him in worship, and He loves it when we spend a whole day in an attitude of rest in Him. Rest for our bodies, and rest for our spirits.

God is very clear: on Sundays, Thou Shalt Do No Chores! It's the longest of the Ten Commandments—like the Good Lord knew we'd need some extra instruction on this one:

Remember the Sabbath day by keeping it holy. Six days you shall labor and do all your work, but the seventh day is a Sabbath to the Lord your God. On it you shall not do any work, neither you, nor your son or daughter, not your manservant or maidservant, nor your animals, nor the alien within your gates. For in six days the Lord made the

heavens and the earth, the sea, and all that is in them, but he
rested on the seventh day. Therefore, the Lord blessed the
Sabbath day and made it holy.

Exodus 20:8-11

That's not a suggestion, is it? It's a commandment, from our
Lord. No work on Sundays. Now, if you're thinking, *But Shannon, I can't not work on Sundays, it would make my Mondays terrible and stress me out for the rest of the week*, I get you. I believe
it's OK for us to keep up with our daily chores and do the basic
things that will give us spiritual clutter if they go undone. God
doesn't want you to feel tense on the Sabbath about what you're
not doing!

Consider what Jesus had to say on the subject. The Phari-
sees, that group of superficial rule-followers and extra-strict rule
makers, accused His disciples of breaking the Sabbath when they
gathered grain to eat. They also accused Jesus Himself of disobey-
ing the fourth commandment when He healed a man on the Sabbath. Consider Jesus' reply:

Then He said to them,
"The Sabbath was made for man, not man for the Sabbath."

Mark 2:27

God tells us to rest from our work on Sundays, not because

it's good for *Him*, but because it's good for *us*. Sundays are for you to declutter your spirit with a time of worship, rest, and peace. So do what is peaceful and restful and joyful to *you*.

I try never to cook on Sundays because I consider it a chore, but my friend Sarah finds joy in cooking big Sunday dinners for her family. I hate shopping for clothes because I find it very frustrating (you petite moms out there can feel my pain—yes, we're very short, but that doesn't necessarily mean we're very old and want to wear dress pants with elastic waists). However, I know there are many, many of you out there, even petites, who love shopping and could make a very successful, restful afternoon out of it.

In the same way, there are things I consider restful which would be chores for another mom. Some of you hate to bake so much you've tried to pass off bakery cookies as your own at a bake sale. To me, devoting a Sunday afternoon to baking chocolate chip cookies—and eating them—would fill up my heart as well as my stomach. I also love to organize things (I can feel your shock from here), so a Sunday afternoon spent blissfully sorting through my wardrobe gives me a delight in the Lord and a thankful heart. Really.

You may feel that even those tasks are not acceptable for Sundays. Follow your faith. You know what an attitude of rest in the Lord means to you. You know what refreshes your spirit.

That's why God made Sundays—for you to connect with Him and rest in His care.

Just plain working

Working Jesus Moms, I hope you've been inspired to apply some of what you've read to your household. Whether you're working full time or part time, in the home or outside of it, you *really* need a chore plan that works for you and your family. Your chore plan may not look exactly like what I've described here, but some of the same principles can still apply.

By grouping your chores together whenever possible and assigning different chores to different days, you *can* make your household run more smoothly. Chore cards can take the guess-work out of what you want to accomplish at home each day. If you work part-time, you can use your chore cards to consolidate chores on your days off, cleaning between loads of laundry or running errands before you catch up on your e-mails.

Full-time working moms may want to divide the most time-consuming chores into sections. If so, you could write "do one load of laundry," "clean one room," "run one errand," or even "write one caring e-mail or note" on daily chore cards. Or you could assign parts of big tasks to specific days, like divvying up your cleaning chores by dusting on Mondays, vacuuming on Tuesdays, cleaning bathrooms on Wednesdays, cleaning the kitchen on Thursdays, and mopping on Fridays. For laundry, you could do whites on Mondays, towels on Tuesdays, brights on Wednesdays, and so on.

Or you could move one or two of The Big Five chores to Saturdays and get your husband and kids involved in completing them. Maybe you'll clean on two Saturdays a month and do laundry on the other two Saturdays. Take a realistic look at your standards to find that "C+ works" level. Don't compare yourself to your other mom friends, figure out what's realistic and achievable for *you*.

Know that God sees you and loves you and still wants you to rest in Him on the Sabbath. If necessary, make Sunday your Project Day, the best "chore" day of the week. Crank up the praise music and find your joy in the Lord as you work to serve your family. And don't forget to indulge in those hobbies sometimes, too... hopefully more Sundays than not. Working Jesus Moms, with a good chore plan *you can still set Sundays apart.*

Hopefully, as you've been reading, you've been applying some of your new time and chore management ideas to your work time and chores, too. You can use organization to clear out your job-related spiritual clutter, becoming a better worker and a better mom. And as a working mom, you have the unique opportunity to *fill up* your spirit at work as well.

When you're at work, allow yourself the joy of serving others in your work capacity with your special skills and abilities. Allow it to be a social outlet by relaxing and enjoying lunch or other breaks with your colleagues. Allow yourself to feel intelligent and capable and special. Embrace whatever it is about your job that makes you a better mom, daughter of God, and blessing to your family.

It's OK to be different

There are also families out there whose work schedules are not Monday through Friday from 8 to 5. My brother-in-law is an intensive care unit nurse, so his family's schedule is always in flux. It's hard for my sister to assign cleaning to Fridays when on some weeks, Friday is their Sunday.

If your schedule is similarly challenging, you can still apply days-of-the-week planning in a more flexible way. Chore cards will help—you can move around your Big Five weekly cards at the beginning of each week to accommodate your family's schedule. You can still have a Laundry Day; the actual day will just change slightly from week to week. You *will* have to do a little more preparation, like buying some extra undies to get you through the weeks when seven days stretch to nine.

No matter what your schedule, it's possible that my Big

Five chore days aren't the right five days for you. Maybe you're a gal who likes to cook freezer meals once a week, so you'd like a Cooking Day. Maybe you want to dedicate a day to your ministry efforts. Maybe you work out of your home and need to assign your chores in a different way. No matter what kind of schedule your family has, you can work your chores into it in the way that works best for *you*.

Your chore plan doesn't have to (and probably won't) look exactly like mine. If you're not loving the chore card idea (what?), you can still find that app. Or you could type up a weekly chore list for your fridge, with tasks assigned to each day of the week. Or you may want to group your big chores together, but do them whenever you feel it's time instead of assigning them to certain days. Just be sure that your chore system is working for you—that you're not letting chore thoughts continue to clutter your spirit.

And no matter what kind of structure (or lack thereof) you prefer, you can free up some time, energy, and brain space by being intentional about doing the chores you want to do as often as you need to do them. Instead of thinking, *I should really...*you'll think, *I will and I am! Thank you, Lord!*

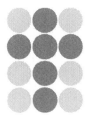

Chapter 6

Chores, Again

Or should I say, more chores.

I'm reading your thoughts. I hear you thinking, *More chores? Really, Shannon?* Only the best kind, Jesus Moms: the ones you almost never have to do.

In the last two chapters, we looked at chores you do over and over again, chores that clutter your spirit because they're always right in front of you. In this chapter, we're going to talk about chores that are easily procrastinated or forgotten. When you *do* remember them, they're a fleeting thought, bugging you with an *I have to remember to...* or worse, stinging you with an *oops, I should have...* These chores are infrequent, but important, so they can still clutter up your spirit with worries that you're not being the Jesus Mom you want to be.

If you're like me, a solid week of that annoying, low-battery chirping from your smoke detector can leave you feeling like a scatterbrained, irresponsible mom. Or maybe you really *meant* to rake the leaves, but before you know it you're looking at your snow-covered lawn with frustration (*ugh, more work for the spring*) and disappointment (*we could've had fun jumping in those leaves!*).

There are all kinds of seasonal chores and maintenance tasks involved in taking care of your home. Even some of your smaller belongings need to be maintained. For example, your vacuum cleaner is supposed to be cleaned out and adjusted every year. (Ever do that? Me neither, but I should. If I did, maybe I wouldn't be on my fourth vacuum cleaner.)

Now, don't let that vacuum cleaner comment send you skimming. Some of you are going to read this chapter and think, *Yes, this is me! This stuff gets away from me,* while others will think, *Eh, I get this stuff done just fine without the extra organization.* If that's you, no problem, but read it anyway just in case. Something might snag your attention and help you to realize that you really could use a reminder or two. You can attach reminders to your Family Calendar, or program them to pop up on your smart phone…or you can use a really consistent, reliable system: your chore box.

By writing your infrequent chores down on monthly chore cards and Monthly Lists, you'll be reminded to complete them at exactly the right time. Both of these organizational tools will help you get your once-in-a-while chores done, and keep them from cluttering your spirit. With this kind of organization, you can let go of these tasks, knowing that you're intentionally doing your best to take care of all that God has given you.

The final chore cards

If you've already started your chore card box, you may be wondering about that "Monthly" section. There are plenty of once-a-month chores that would be perfect for chore cards! Try thinking through each of your Big Five chores and reading over your Goal List to help you discover once-a-month tasks that are important to you. Write a fat capital "M" on each of these index card strips to remind you to return them to the monthly section. (More about how to remember to use your monthly cards is coming up in Chapter 7.)

Only you know what monthly chores are necessary for you, but I'll share some of the things that work for me to help get you thinking. I'd start with Cleaning Day, but I'm sure plenty of monthly cleaning chores are springing to mind without my help. (This means that I'm actually too embarrassed to tell you the things I only clean once a month, lest you think me a poor house-keeper. I'm not kidding about doing chores as little as possible! You can check out Appendix D for a few ideas.)

One Errand Day a month, I do a quick clean-out of my purse and our car, which is yucky but necessary. I once participated in a Mothers of Preschoolers scavenger hunt where the only rule was that we had to procure the list of items from our purses and cars. One of the items on the list was "an old French fry" and there were plenty of moms who found them. One mom asked if an old chicken nugget counted. This was one game I was actually thankful to lose!

Though my car is relatively tidy, I do keep a box of books and activities there for the kids to enjoy when we're driving around—especially when we're running errands. One Errand Day a month, I take the box of goodies inside and swap them out for new things to keep the kids happy. (They always notice it right away!) I also sort through my coupons, tossing the expired ones and refreshing my memory about those deals.

On the first Communication Day of the month, I intentionally strengthen my relationships. First, I look at the upcoming month on our Family Calendar and choose two date nights: one with my hubby, and one with one of my kids.

We Jesus Moms know that we should date our husbands—a million marriage books can't be wrong! Even though I can be quite frugal (a word which sounds ever so much nicer than "cheap"), I know that nights out with Travis are fun and refreshing. They connect us in a way that watching TV on the couch never will. Even so, if I'm not intentional about scheduling a sitter and getting us out the door, it never happens.

We don't often luck into special quality time with our kids, either. Travis and I purposefully rotate "kid dates" so that each child goes out individually with each parent before the cycle starts over. The kid of the night gets to choose a restaurant and activity to share with Mom or Dad. On my nights out with the kids, I subtly (or not-so-subtly) pump them for information: what they're thinking and feeling about school, their friends, our family, Jesus, you name it. It's a precious time to connect.

Once a month on Communication Day, I also do a "relationship check," glancing through my paper and e-mail address books. I may be reminded of someone who could use the boost of a "thinking of you" greeting card, or decide to invite a friend I haven't seen in a while out for dessert (I don't do coffee—where's the chocolate in that?). I may remember to check a friend's blog so I can keep up with her news, or invite a family we want to get to know better over for pizza. I also make sure that I have plans to call or visit my three amazing grandparents sometime during the month. In all of these ways, I'm consciously choosing to share a little of God's love with my family and friends, keeping our relationships strong.

On Project Day, a.k.a. You Day, I make sure that I'm taking care of myself. I throw out my disposable contacts and put in new ones. I renew our family's prescriptions, and do a self breast exam. (That may be too much information, but I'm including it because it's important for all of us moms.) I even treat myself to a good exfoliating foot scrub. Undoubtedly, you'll have your own ideas about how best to take care of—and treat!—yourself on this special day.

These are only a few of the chores and tasks you might want to complete once a month. Appendix D has more examples, but your daily, weekly, and monthly chore cards are going to be uniquely *you*. Remember, you're doing what you *want* to do as often as you *need* to do it. Many of these chores can be done every other month and still leave you feeling completely satisfied. (You can draw a star on your every-other-month chore cards just as you did for your every-other-week cards.) You're the only one who knows what you need to accomplish to be the best mom and daughter of God you can be.

Chores that almost never need done (the best kind)

Speaking of doing chores as little as possible, what about the chores you want to do once a quarter, or once every six months, or even once a year? Since these things aren't so repetitive, don't bother making chore cards for them. Instead, write a list of chores for each calendar month on twelve index cards, and store them in the "Monthly List" section in your box. You can use these lists year after year to remind you what you'd like to accomplish each month. (I'll give a more detailed account about how to pull your time and chore management tools together into one great system at the end of the next chapter.)

Some of the things you write on your Monthly Lists may be inspired by your Goal List or Greater To-Do List. You can check out Appendix B for ways to use monthly chore cards and your Monthly Lists to help you reach your goals. You'll also think of tasks you want to do *this* year, but not every year. If you'd like to remember to do something this August alone, write it on a Post-it note and stick it to the Monthly List. That way, you can forget all about it until August rolls around. After writing these tasks down, you'll feel so organized and be able to let them go!

Seasonal and holiday related chores need to be done during certain months, so write those down first. After writing these tasks on your Monthly Lists, some months will already look pretty full. (Do I hear December?) You should also think about which of your months will be especially hopping for you because of things like sport seasons, demanding periods at work, or busy spells in your ministries. The months that don't have as much on them are the months to schedule the infrequent chores that can be done any-time. Don't overload any one month—writing down these chores is supposed to help you relax, not stress you out!

Your Monthly Lists are there to help you keep track of your infrequent chores and to help you accomplish your goals. I've got plenty of ideas about what you may want to write on these lists coming up in this chapter and the next, and I've got some sample Monthly Lists for you in Appendix E. Just keep in mind that Monthly Lists are really individual things—you should consider whether or not you have spiritual clutter about each topic, and then decide what tasks you'd like to add to your lists.

To everything there is a season

Seasonal chores are easy to put off…until the weather changes, and then it's too late. To avoid that kind of spiritual clutter, you should start off your Monthly Lists by writing down the seasonal chores that need to be accomplished during certain months. If you plan for them, you'll be the neighbor we all wish we had!

If you own a home, you'll need to get ready to mow your yard in the spring, so make a note on your April list to buy lawn bags and gasoline for the mower. You may want to stain your fence or deck, schedule a mulch delivery, and take your lawn mower in for yearly maintenance as well. Later in the spring, you may want to remind yourself to trim bushes, mulch flowerbeds, and plant flowers. When the time comes, you can schedule these chores on Saturdays so the whole family can get involved.

On a fall Monthly List, you may want to write a reminder to clean up your landscaping and "winterize" around your house. Cut back perennials, rake leaves, unhook hoses from spigots, check the weather stripping around your windows, and cover your outdoor furniture or move it inside. You'll decrease your energy bills and save money and hassle by protecting your home and belongings.

Looking *mah*-velous

Spring and fall weather can sneak up on you in another way: the weather changes, and suddenly your kids don't have anything to wear! Make a note on your April and September Monthly Lists to remind you to tackle your clothing chores. You'll need to donate, sell, or store outgrown clothing, sort through hand-me-downs, and decide what you need to purchase for the next season. Don't forget to think about things like coats, hats and mittens, shoes, socks, underwear, and even hair accessories for your girly girls.

This is one of those tasks where an "I *get* to do this" attitude makes a big difference. I make buying new clothes more fun for my kids (and for me) by planning a Kid Date Night Shopping Extravaganza. I ease them into the evening by letting the kid of the night choose where we eat dinner, then we hit the racks. Shopping with one kid at a time is a much calmer experience than trying to choose clothes for multiple kids at once. I can really focus on each child, discern their individual tastes, and make wise purchases.

Wardrobes can cause a lot of spiritual clutter. If you avoid dealing with your kids' clothes, or simply forget to until after the weather changes, you'll end up worrying that they're too hot or too cold, or that they look like ragamuffins in clothes that don't fit. It's not superficial to want your kids to look nice and feel comfortable in what they're wearing. It just makes sense.

In the same way, Jesus Moms, it's not superficial to put a little thought into what *you're* wearing. If you feel unattractive in your chosen outfit, you'll clutter your spirit with negative thoughts all day. Moms deserve to feel good about themselves, inside and out. As my friend Susan told me, it takes the same amount of time to put on a cute top and a stylish pair of jeans as it takes to pull on a t-shirt and sweatpants—so why not decide to feel good about how you look? I'm not saying you need to spend a ton of time and money putting together a fabulous wardrobe. I'm saying you should love yourself (and your husband!) enough to dress in a way that makes you feel attractive.

Take the time to make sure everything fits you and is still in style—even your coats, shoes, jewelry, and other accessories.

Consider how many and what kind of outfits you'd like for work, church, social events, and quiet days at home. Make a shopping list of items you need to complete your wardrobe, and get yourself to a mall. (I know most of you think that's fun!) By writing wardrobe reminders on your Monthly Lists, you'll keep up with the changing styles and the changing seasons.

Just whistle while you work

Now, not all chores are seasonal. Spring Cleaning doesn't have to happen in the spring! In fact, once or twice a year cleaning chores are great fillers for those lighter months without big holidays, like January, June and August. Here are a few things you may want to do between one and four times a year (as infrequently as you feel the need to):

- Clean out your refrigerator, freezer, and pantry
- Clean your stove and other kitchen appliances
- Dust high ledges and ceiling fans
- Clean blinds and other window treatments
- Wipe off woodwork
- Remove marks from walls and doors
- Wash windows, inside and out
- Clean and disinfect toys
- Straighten and clean your garage
- Straighten and clean your basement
- Change your furnace filters

- Beat or wash rugs
- Thoroughly clean pet areas
- Clean your laundry baskets with disinfecting wipes
- Turn mattresses
- Straighten closets and drawers
- Any other deep cleaning that comes to mind

Go ahead and take a walk around your house, inside and out, to see what kind of "spring" cleaning chores you can come up with. This is the time to consider your belongings as well. Some of them may require yearly maintenance, like that vacuum cleaner I mentioned. Well, maybe "require" is too strong a word, but you should consider the suggested maintenance for your belongings to keep them working longer and better for you.

Don't forget your car—make notes on your Monthly Lists to remind yourself to get the oil changed, fill up on antifreeze and windshield wiper fluid, and do all of those other car things I don't know anything about. (I'm not a car girl.)

You'll probably want to "clean out" some other things as well. You can use your Monthly Lists to remind yourself to delete some of the saved messages in your e-mail account, or review your list of contacts in order to get rid of any out-dated information. On your February or March list, you should write yourself a reminder to get started on your taxes and clear out your files, tossing old paperwork, bills, and receipts.

If you think of any seasonal cleaning tasks, write those things on your Monthly Lists first. Then, fill in the lighter months with the non-seasonal cleaning tasks. When you spread them out, they don't seem so overwhelming—and you'll never worry that it's been *way* too long since you last did them.

Growing healthy and strong

Some of your most important once or twice a year to-dos involve your family's health. On one or two Monthly Lists, remind yourself to raid your medicine cabinet. Toss expired medications, and replace them by renewing your prescriptions and adding over-the-counter medications to your shopping list. If you have family members with allergies, you may also want to schedule cleanings for air ducts and carpeting.

Be intentional about making checkup appointments for your kids, yourself, and your husband with your dentist, eye doctor, and family doctor or pediatrician. Make appointments for yourself at the OBGYN and any other specialists you should be consulting. You can make a note on your September or October Monthly List to see about getting flu shots. If you have pets, schedule checkups and shots for them, too.

For these yearly appointments, be sure to write your reminders on the Monthly Lists that are two or three months *before* you want the actual appointment, giving your doctors ample time to get you scheduled. Don't let any should-dos about your health and the health of other family members leave you with a sense of unease. Use your Monthly Lists to keep yourself, your kids, and your husband going healthy and strong.

Stop, drop, and plan

Jesus Moms, you don't need the spiritual clutter of worrying about your kids' safety, either. Entrust them to God, and do what you can to keep them safe. For starters, decide when you want to change the batteries in your smoke and carbon monoxide detectors and write reminders on your individual Monthly Lists. Then, take it up a notch by choosing two or three times a year to talk with your kids about fire safety, stranger danger, and other safety topics.

None of us really want to spend time thinking about these scary issues, but you can make it as fun as possible for your kids while still conveying the necessary information. Spencer and Karly have fun critiquing each other's "stop, drop, and roll" form, and they love to "get low and go" during our family fire drills. They laugh as they take turns being dragged out of our family room "store," kicking, hitting, and shouting "You're not my mom!" or "You're not my dad!" as loud as they can (Spencer actually gave me a puffy eye once). I pretend to be a stranger offering them candy or asking for help with the puppies in my car, and once they've said "No" and run a few times, I get more and more outrageous with my fake offer. ("But I've got a baby *elephant* in there!")

We get more serious as we talk about running from guns if their friends want to show them one. We talk about how it's OK to "tattle" on someone if there's any chance they might get hurt or hurt someone else. We discuss how they should stick with their buddies so they're not alone with unfamiliar grown-ups. I make sure they know we don't have secrets in our family (unless they're fun surprise secrets like presents), and that they could tell me *anything* and I'd never, ever love them any less.

I know this isn't fun stuff to discuss, but you'll have the special peace that comes from knowing you're doing the best you can to keep your kids safe. It's scary to dwell on how many of these things are out of our control, but we can give our worries to the Lord by lifting our kids' safety up in prayer. To help me, I've printed out part of a psalm of David and put it on my nightstand:

> I will lie down and sleep in peace,
> For you alone, O Lord,
> Make me dwell in safety.
>
> *-Psalm 4:8*

I read it almost every night before I turn out the light, and it gives me so much peace. Jesus Moms, safety doesn't come from being inside our homes with our doors securely locked, or from putting fire drills on our Monthly Lists. We can—and should—be intentional and do our best to keep our family members safe, but it's the Lord who makes us dwell in safety. We can rest in Him.

My second favorite before-bed verse, brought to my attention by my friend Jessica, is also a psalm:

> Be at rest once more, oh my soul,
> for the Lord has been good to you.
>
> *Psalm 116:7*

Jesus Moms, the Lord has been so very good to us! Every one of the once-in-a-while chores we've been considering in this chapter stems from the blessings of home and family our Lord has given us. When we write down those infrequent chores on monthly chore cards or individual Monthly Lists, we're clearing out our spiritual clutter about what we "should" be doing so we can let those things go. Our souls can be at rest in the Lord as we enjoy our family and home, being the Jesus Moms we want to be!

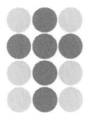

Chapter 7

Planning for Fun

So we're done talking about chores…or are we? Sadly, family activities and events that should be fun often turn into dreaded chores. Holiday fun, especially, can be ruined by an ill-prepared, stressed-out mom. If you don't plan ahead for those fun times, you end up feeling hassled and rushed and far from what you'd like to feel: joyful in the Lord!

Consider dyeing and decorating Easter eggs with your kids. You suddenly realize that Easter is tomorrow (already?!?), so you rush to the store to pick up eggs and a dyeing kit. You get home and boil your eggs, only to realize that you don't have enough vinegar for the dye tablets—back to the store you go. By the time you're actually coloring the eggs, you're feeling harried, the kids are getting tired, and no one is really enjoying themselves.

Coloring Easter eggs is supposed to be so much fun, but this year, even though you "got them done," you really missed the boat. If only you'd thought through your Easter egg tradition earlier in the week, purchasing supplies ahead of time and choosing the best day and time for your decorating party. With a little planning, you could've laid the foundation for a fun celebration of the Lord's resurrection and talked about new life in Him...and made a happy memory for your family.

One of my favorite movie moments is in *Hook*, a sequel of sorts to the Peter Pan stories. As the movie opens, we discover that Peter is a grown-up pirate—a workaholic who misses his son's big baseball game and then starts working his way through a family vacation. He is, in fact, working his way through something Peter Pan should know is precious: his kids' childhood. His wife confronts him with the perfect combination of frustration and love. After tossing his cell phone out a window (and looking shocked that she did it), she quietly says to him, "So *fast*, Peter. It's a few years, then it's over. And you are not being careful. *And you are missing it.*" (I get misty-eyed every time. Shoot, I'm tearing up right now.)

Even the best, most Christ-centered moms kick themselves for missing it sometimes. Life can sneak up on us. We miss great opportunities to love and enjoy our kids, just because we aren't being careful.

I'm passionate about calling moms to live with intention (hopefully, you've figured this out by now). Jesus Moms, it's not enough to think, *Oh yeah, that'd be a great thing to do, I should totally do that.* You have to make the decision to do it and be intentional about getting it done…and truly enjoying it.

The answer is *not* working more or working harder. The key is deciding what's important to you, and writing it down so you remember to actually do it. That's why I've been telling you about planners, calendars, chore cards, and Monthly Lists. You're not just organizing your time, you're organizing your *life*.

Jesus Moms, the Lord has blessed us with so much, and, with intention, we can be fantastic stewards of those blessings. So don't put away those Monthly Lists yet! In this chapter, we're going to talk about holidays and birthdays and toys and pictures and all kinds of fun stuff. Your Monthly Lists will help you to plan and prepare so that you can relax and savor those God-given moments of blessing when they come.

A jolly holiday with Mommy

In most homes, we moms are the ones in charge of holiday traditions. Santa gets all the press, but most often, it's Mrs. Claus running the show: decorating, baking, shopping, wrapping, and making it all as fun as possible! Moms make holidays happen, and that takes planning. Each holiday involves different—and hopefully enjoyable—tasks we need to remember.

I'm all about holidays—we have special traditions for almost every holiday on the calendar! Most of them stem from my childhood, but I've also embraced the traditions my husband remembers with nostalgia. And I'm always on the look-out for new holiday activities—you know, copying my friends' holiday traditions, scouring *Family Fun* magazine, and becoming addicted to Pinterest. (As a completely non-creative person, I need to poach other people's ideas.)

Most importantly, I'm always looking for ways to center every holiday around Jesus, so all of our family celebrations are fundamentally times of thanksgiving to our Lord for all He's done for us. For example, The Uptons talk about God's blessings every St. Patrick's Day. As a former Kelley, I make it a point to celebrate the man who brought the Good News about Jesus to Ireland.

Each year, I decorate the house in green, bake traditional Irish soda bread, and often host the annual Kelley Family St. Patty's Day Jig Fest. We all drink green 7Up, eat way too many shamrock cookies, and delight in fake-jigging with our kids (my friend Sarah pointed out that our dancing is actually more reminiscent of a Polka than a Jig…but we don't care). We have a great, completely silly time, and the kids have a ball seeing the grown-ups cut loose a bit.

Since my kids say that I'm the "serious" parent, I try to prove them wrong by celebrating even the smaller, sillier holidays. For example, I have a note on my March Monthly List to remind myself to make plans to fool my kids and/or husband on April 1st. I love to say "April Fools!" after a really good trick or surprise. And I almost always get them, because they don't expect things like that from Serious Mom!

Family holidays are the perfect excuse for Jesus Moms to delight in our loved ones and strengthen our family bond—and you can make any day a reason to celebrate. No matter where you live, there's a day set aside to celebrate almost everything: National Whatever's Day. Though some of them are ridiculous (do we *need* to have National Towel Day?), some of them can start a new tradition in your family. For example, my kids write notes and draw pictures for their cousins on July 24th, the USA's National Cousins Day. What a great excuse for a kid to get mail!

You could even make up a holiday during a humdrum month. Have a birthday party for your pet. Plan a "red day" when your family members are required to wear red and eat only red food for dinner. Be creative and bring your family closer together. Who knows, you may even find a way to celebrate National Towel Day.

When you're writing your Monthly Lists, consider exactly what you want to do in order to make each holiday a special, spiritual time of celebration for you and your family. Love your husband by continuing the traditions he holds dear. If you'd like to try out a new idea or start a new tradition, write those things on your Monthly Lists as well (but in pencil, you know, in case the activity bombs).

Be sure to take into account the differences in the calendar each year, like the number of days between Thanksgiving and Christmas, or the timing of Easter Sunday. Easter activities are on my March list just so I don't forget them, but if Easter is later in the year, I push those to-dos back into April. (After all, I don't want to gloss over St. Patrick's Day!)

When you review your Monthly Lists, you can decide which holiday activities will require to-dos on your daily planner pages, and which will be better served with time blocked out on your Family Calendar. Planning ahead for these events will ensure that they actually happen, and will allow you to enjoy them even more. Party on!

Baby, let the good times roll

While we're discussing celebrations, I have to give special mention to birthdays. Once a year, the Lord hands you a day to celebrate the gift of a cherished person—what an honor! When you review your calendar each month, make a note on your shopping list to buy cards or gifts for any upcoming birthdays. In your planner, on the daily to-do lists that are three or four days before each birthday (or on your Communication Day for that week), write to-dos that will remind you to send them. Or write a reminder to call and sing "Happy Birthday" or send an e-mail to let the birthday person know you're thinking of them.

For Jesus Moms, our children's birthdays are extra special days. We celebrate that they're a year older while secretly mourning that another age has passed. We remember the day of their birth, but try desperately not to remember the actual labor and delivery (well, maybe that's just me). Adoptive moms remember "Gotcha Days." No matter how our children came to us, tears come to our eyes as we recall the sheer joy of holding them for the first time. We send up prayers of praise and thanksgiving for our children, the precious blessings the Lord has entrusted to us.

What an opportunity to lavish love on our kids! Everyone has different birthday traditions, and they can require a lot of planning. On the appropriate Monthly Lists, I've written reminders to book portrait sittings, shop for gifts, and start to plan the parties well in advance (I do *love* a good at-home birthday party). I write reminders to take pictures and shoot a little video of the birthday kid. I also interview each little Upton on their actual birthdays, quizzing them about their current "favorites": favorite food, favorite place to go for fun, favorite anything I can think of. I include these fun lists in our family scrapbooks.

A little pre-planning can take the "chore" out of loving up your kids on their birthdays. You don't want to be hurried and hassled on their big days, you want to celebrate and soak in the moment. You know how you most enjoy making your kids' birthdays special with your own traditions, so write birthday-related tasks on your Monthly Lists to help you to relax and enjoy your child's special day.

The fun stuff—toys

Birthdays are huge reminders that our kids are growing up. There are a couple of practical issues to deal with as our kids get bigger, like outgrown clothes and toys. While the changing seasons and constantly growing kids practically force you to deal with the clothes, the toys can get really out of hand if you don't intentionally sort through them on a regular basis.

Toys are fun…until they start to overwhelm your home and clutter your spirit with frustration. They multiply in ways I don't fully understand. When Spencer was a newborn, every one of his toys fit into a small basket. By the time Oliver was born, our "age 0 to 6 months" toys took up eight small toy bins and most of a good-size toy box. All of those toys for a little person who just lies down or sits in one spot, looking around and chewing on stuff!

It gets worse as they get older. The appropriate age range for toys gets bigger and bigger until you reach the infinity of "ages 8 and up." No longer can you point to the age on the box and say, "Honey, you're just getting too big for this." And kids can find a way to play with any toy you're even thinking about getting rid of. All you need to do is look at a toy and think, *They're not playing with that any more...time to let it go,* and instantly your kids begin to play with it in new and creative ways. They'll hear your thoughts and come running from different parts of the house. They can hear those thoughts at *school.* Time to get rid of their stuff? No way.

Whether they realize it or not, kids can be overwhelmed with too many toys and end up not playing with most of them. Your house can get overwhelmed with them as well. Lots of moms try to avoid this by putting toys into rotation, stowing some away for a while, and then getting them back out. If you're one of those moms, then you can use your Monthly Lists to remind you to get the toys out of the basement before your kids are too old to really enjoy them.

I'm more of a tosser by nature. Actually, I've put most of our outgrown toys into storage for younger siblings (which is proba-bly why Oliver's toys could fill up an entire room at this point). I'll admit it: I have a hard time letting them go. Moms in our gen-eration have all seen *Toy Story* a time or two, so we may need to remind ourselves that toys don't actually have feelings. They're transient belongings, and it's a positive thing when our kids mature and outgrow them.

Soon Oliver is going to start out-growing his toys, too, so I know I'll be letting go of more and more. I am planning to keep some of my very, very favorite toys for my grandkids, though. My mom did that, and I've had such a wonderful time sharing my old Legos and Pretty Ponies with Spencer and Karly. I'm already looking forward to playing with some of my kids' toys again, sharing them with my grandkids when the time comes.

You can use your Monthly Lists to remind yourself to sort through the toys two or three times a year. Some great times of year to tackle this chore are just before or after Christmas, after your kids' birthdays, or when school's about to start. Weed out the ones that are broken, no longer age-appropriate, or just unused. If your kids aren't really enjoying a toy, let it go to a kid who will love it.

As your kids get older, you can include them in the sorting process.[1] You should lay out some ground rules right at the start—most importantly, Mom has the Final Word on what stays and what goes. You can teach your kids to keep themselves organized by challenging *them* to figure out what will fit in their closets. You

---

1 To get your kids involved in a fun way, check out the article "The Toy Challenge" on OrganizingJesusMoms.com.

can also foster their charitable Jesus hearts by encouraging them to give their toys away to other kids.

If your kids are teenagers, they need to toss their own stuff. It's time for them to learn to manage their own time and belongings. I don't have any teenagers of my own yet, but I did teach a bunch of them math for a while, and I know they can be a bit prickly about this topic. (Understatement?) Some of the high schoolers I taught were very organized, but some of them had several dogs eating their homework.

Your teenagers will only live at home for a few more precious years (or so you hope), so this is the time to help them discover organization and its benefits. You can use many of the principles in this book, or look for organizational books for teens and planners designed for students. Think of their future college roommates. Think of their future *spouses*. Later in life, your children (and all of the people they ever live with) will thank you for helping them to become functionally organized people.

Capturing the fun on film (well, in megabytes)

But let's not get ahead of ourselves. Before we send our kids out into the world, we want to take lots and lots of pictures of them! Often, moms are the family historians, the ones who turn the family fun into tangible memories we can enjoy again and again. You can use your Monthly Lists to remind you to take your camera to your special events. If you want to take more pictures of your everyday activities, write a weekly or monthly chore card that simply says "take pictures of something fun." [2]

And don't forget to actually enjoy the pictures! If it would help you, write a monthly chore card, or a reminder on a few of your Monthly Lists, to get those pictures off of your camera's rapidly filling memory card. Upload them to your computer, post them, and order photo prints as often as you need to in order to avoid getting overwhelmed.

You may also want to write a reminder on one or two Monthly Lists to put together photo albums or family scrapbooks. Decide how frequently you'd like to set aside the time to fill in your kids' baby books, or spend some time journaling about each of your children.[3] Even if you're not a scrapbooker, your kids will love looking through your family photo albums—especially those crazy-hair and goofy-smile pictures—and reading the things you've written about them.

You can also make notes on your Monthly Lists reminding

2 For a great list of everyday pictures to take, check out the "Everyday Photo Ideas" article on OrganizingJesusMoms.com.

3 Yes, I'm recommending another OrganizingJesusMoms.com article, this one called "Joyful Journaling." (I just couldn't fit everything into the book!)

you to encourage other family members to write. Older kids can write a little about themselves on their birthdays or at the end of each school year. You may need to suggest some topics to get them started—school, friends, favorite toys or games—whatever you'd like them to share. You'll gain insight into their hearts and minds, and precious keepsakes to treasure.

Jesus Moms, we all feel a little panic sometimes about how fast this time with our kids is flying by. But when you're organized, you can let that feeling of panic subside into the knowledge that *you aren't missing it*. As you write your Monthly Lists, you're making your growing kids and family traditions priorities in your life. And when the time comes, you'll be able to complete these tasks with joy in Jesus! You'll intentionally enjoy your time with your kids, soak up God's blessings, and make memories that will last forever—even into eternity.

All together now

OK, so now you have a planner, a Family Calendar, chore cards for daily, weekly, and monthly tasks, and twelve individual Monthly Lists of things to do. Whew, great planning, Jesus Moms! Let's bring them all together into one great system that will save you time and clear out your spiritual clutter. If you're ready to try this system, take a good look at Appendix A—it's a "cheat sheet" of sorts for your Daily and Monthly Planning times, and a guide to reviewing your goals. (If you're making your own system, reading through this section may give you ideas for incorporating Daily and Monthly Planning and Goal Reviews into your way of doing things.)

For Daily Planning, you should spend five to ten minutes at night or in the morning prayerfully planning for the upcoming day—in just a few minutes, God can bring such peace to your spirit. Check your calendar, prioritize the to-dos in your planner, and lay out your white daily and colored day-of-the-week chore cards. (If you'd like an actual picture of this, check out Appendix C.) Then take a moment to give your whole day over to God, asking for His divine guidance and His blessing on the work you're doing for your family and for Him.

Once a month, you'll need to set aside about twenty to thirty minutes for Monthly Planning. Write a monthly chore card that says "Choose a date for Monthly Planning." As you plan for the upcoming month, that chore card will prompt you to schedule the *next* Monthly Planning time so you can keep yourself planning! I like to schedule my Monthly Planning time at the end of the month—usually my last Communication Day—so I'm prepared in advance for the upcoming month.

For Monthly Planning, sit down at your favorite workspace with your planner, Family Calendar, and chore card box with the appropriate Monthly List. If you've purchased a planner with re-fill pages, add the pages for the approaching month (you'll want to keep two to three months-worth of pages for your planner so you can look ahead and refer back to previous days). Surrounded by your time and chore management tools, you'll be ready to plan for the month ahead. This is a great time to lift your heart up to the Lord and ask for clarity and wisdom as you plan the next month for your family.

Open your planner to the first day of the new month, turn over the page in your Family Calendar to the same month, and sync them up. (Did you see how I used some technical lingo there? Oh yeah.) As you look at the events on your calendar, write any tasks related to those events on the daily to-do lists in your planner. You can plan for all of your imminent birthdays, holidays, and events this way. By looking at the month as a whole, and keeping your chore days in mind, you can choose the best days to complete your upcoming tasks.

Next, look at the individual Monthly List, including any Post-it notes you've added about things specifically for this year. Write any associated tasks on your daily to-do lists, or schedule specific times to accomplish them on your Family Calendar. Since these chores are done so infrequently, you can look for days that are really convenient, and spread them out through the month.

Finally, distribute your monthly chore cards into the appropriate days-of-the-week sections for the next week. Try to match like chores so you can do them efficiently—monthly cleaning chores on Cleaning Day, monthly communication chores on Communication Day, and so on. If a chore doesn't really fit into one of your Big Five categories, assign it to a "lighter" chore day.

Each day of the upcoming week, you'll lay out your monthly chore cards with your daily and weekly cards in their appropriate time chunks. Just like daily and weekly chores, they're usually "2" priority tasks. By the end of the week, you'll have replaced your monthly cards in the monthly section, ready to be forgotten until the next month.

This whole planner/calendar/card review process only takes about twenty minutes a month, but the planning time is invaluable. As you're hanging your calendar back on the wall and replacing your planner and chore card box nearby, you'll feel incredibly prepared for the month ahead. With your organizational system, you'll be ready to do what you *need* to do, and what you *want* to do as well.

Keeping your goals in sight

In addition, you should do a Goal Review two to four times a year. Decide how often you'd like to do this and write "Goal Review" on a few Monthly Lists. You'll do the Goal Review as a part of your Monthly Planning time, adding about thirty minutes to the process—and it will be worth it! You'll remind yourself of the reasons why you're doing what you're doing, and you'll be able to see the progress you're making toward your goals. You may even get to cross some off—job well done!

As you prayerfully review your Goal List, you may decide some of the goals you'd previously written aren't for you after all, or maybe just not for right now. On the other hand, maybe the time has come to begin to work toward one of the "future" goals on your Greater To-Do List. As you think through your relationships, personal dreams, and callings, you may think of brand new goals. Ask the Lord for His leading about how you're choosing to spend your time and energy, and then write a new, updated Goal List.

Then, use your planning system to help you reach your goals. Consider how you want to use your daily to-do lists, the note space in your planner, your Family Calendar, your daily and monthly chore cards, and your Monthly Lists to help you complete each one. For a few examples of how all of your organizational tools can help you reach your goals, check out Appendix B.

After you've considered your goals, you should update your chore cards and Monthly Lists. Once you've used a daily chore card for a while, you may realize it's become a habit and you no longer need the card to remind you. And you may realize you don't need to do some chores as often as you'd thought, so you can "demote" them—a weekly chore to an every-other weekly, an every-other weekly to a monthly, and so on. (How I love doing that.)

Your chores will change with your family's schedule as well, especially in September and June. Each school year brings new activity schedules and weekly routines for your family, and summer vacation means setting up a whole new daily routine for you and your kids. You may want to move your chores to different days of the week in order to accommodate your new family schedule.

After you've reviewed your Goal List and your chore box, you can complete your Monthly Planning as usual. Remember, you can always use Appendix A to guide you through these steps. With Goal Reviews, Monthly Planning sessions, and a few minutes a day dedicated to Daily Planning, you'll clear out your spiritual clutter and organize *you*.

Being the Jesus Mom you want to be

Now, I know this is a lot of structure and it may not be for everyone. I've already said that I highly recommend a list of goals and a daily planner to hold your to-do lists—those are the bare minimum organizational tools for any mom out there. Beyond that, only you know what systems will best help you to take care of your family and clear out your spiritual clutter.

If you're not going to do it the way I've laid out, then how *are* you going to do it? You've got to come up with a system that really works for your household. *Please* take some prayerful time to consider what you've read and decide which of these ideas you want to incorporate into your way of doing things. Figure out how you're going to keep yourself accountable and keep your systems working for you.

Of course, I'd love it if you'd give my whole system a try and I encourage you to do so. But my real prayer is that this book inspires you to be *intentional* about how you're choosing to spend your time and live your life as a mom. When you choose to organize your time, you're choosing to build your house minute by minute, hour by hour, and day by day.

I've mentioned the Proverbs 31 woman several times, the biblical Wife of Noble Character described at the very end of the book of Proverbs. If anyone is organized, she is. *She's* giving thought to her ways and building her home with both hands. Here are some of the descriptions of her:

> She sets about her work vigorously;
> her arms are strong for her tasks.
> She sees that her trading is profitable,
> and her lamp does not go out at night.
>
> *(vs 17 & 18)*

When it snows, she has no fear for her household;

for all of them are clothed in scarlet.

She is clothed with strength and dignity;

she can laugh at the days to come.

(vs 21 & 25)

She watches over the affairs of her household

and does not eat the bread of idleness.

Her children arise and call her blessed;

her husband also, and he praises her.

(vs 27 & 28)

Jesus Moms, this is what we're working to become. We want to work hard and plan ahead. We want to know that we're prepared for the future and look forward to each day. We want to watch over the affairs of our households and be the pride of our husbands and children. *We want to bring glory to God with our lives.* And hopefully, you now have a very clear sense of how to begin achieving those things.

In the last few chapters, you've considered the work you'd like to do to build your house for your family. You've written your goals and identified the first steps toward completing them. You've made a chore plan that involves fewer chores and more time for you. You've reviewed all of your responsibilities as a mom and chosen to do the things that matter, the things that will help you to be the Jesus Mom and the woman of God you want to be.

Jesus Moms, God has given you these hours, days, months, and years with your husband and children as a precious gift. You *know* what you want to do with God's gift of time now, and you're being intentional about doing those things. You can wake up each day ready to accomplish your goals with your mind and body, and with your heart truly resting in Jesus.

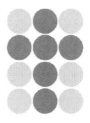

Chapter 8

Loving Lists

Alright, so you've got a great handle on your time, chores, and activities. You've organized them, and you know exactly what you want to *do*. Now we're going to tackle what you want to *think*.

With these last few chapters, we're going to organize your thoughts. Yes, your *thoughts*. This is the epitome of clearing out mental clutter! We all think random things—often important or creative ideas—we'd like to remember, only to lose them a few moments later.

Imagine with me that you bring your favorite, yummy-gooey homemade dessert to an evening Bible study. A friend gushes about how much she loves it and asks you for the recipe. You're flattered and assure her you'll e-mail it to her as soon as you get home. You really intend to. But by the time you get home, it's getting late and you jump straight into tuck-in mode with your kids instead.

A few days later, you're in the middle of making dinner when you remember her compliment and realize you've forgotten to e-mail her the recipe. You can't do it right then without burning dinner, so you stir and think, *I've got to remember to do that!* But by the time you're setting the table, it's forgotten again.

Before you know it, you're bumping into that friend at church and thinking, *I wonder if she remembers that I forgot to give her that recipe.* Well, she might remember and think you're being a secretive yummy-gooey recipe hoarder. (We all know one or two of those.) Or she might realize you've just forgotten and graciously remind you, which puts you right back where you started. Or she might have forgotten all about it herself!

Your spirit doesn't have to be cluttered with those *I've got to remember* and *I know I have that written down somewhere around here* thoughts. You can intentionally avoid that kind of frustration and quiet the nagging thoughts that repeat like a melody you can't quite get out of your head—*I should ask Mom about that... Oh, right, I need to call Mom and ask her about that... I have got to call Mom about that!* Frazzled, harried thoughts like these just distract us from what's important—living our lives for our Savior, in His peace and presence.

With a little organization, you can get control over your thoughts and ideas. Jesus Moms, I'm sure you can guess by now what my solution to this spiritual clutter will be—it is pretty simple. When you have a great thought or idea you'd like to remember, *write it down.* The minute it's on paper, your mind will let it go, and your spirit will relax.

Writing down these fleeting thoughts will keep your mind organized, and your spirit clutter free, in a different way than planning does. Some things you can't plan for ahead of time—you have to wait for inspiration! The Holy Spirit can whisper to us in quiet moments, and we don't want to miss it by being distracted or hurried.

You can contain your inspired thoughts and nagging to-dos in your new organizational system by adding some lists—how I love them! When my husband isn't calling me "Shan with a Plan," he's usually calling me "List Lady." I think I have a list to hold every thought that comes into my head—and you can, too. In this chapter and the next, we'll talk about the kinds of lists you may want to keep, and how to make them accessible enough for you to really use them.

Any mom can make and keep some good, basic lists in order to organize her thoughts. I know Type-A Moms love them, and the slightly less-structured moms out there probably enjoy a good list, too. If your purse is filled with random jottings on receipts and flyers, then you're a list-lover in disguise. You're probably at least halfway there already—those little pieces of paper covering your countertops, Post-it notes stuck all over your refrigerator, and random reminders on your smart phone are lists just waiting to happen.

Even the Lord loves lists! From the first genealogy in Genesis to the Book of Life in Revelation, the Lord speaks to us through lists. The Old Testament contains many detailed lists of laws and guidelines for the Hebrew people, including the Big List: the Ten Commandments. In the New Testament we find the Beatitudes, the fruits of the spirit, and the list of the faithful in Hebrews 11. God wrote lists in the Bible for us to read, understand, and learn, so He must have created us to sort and store information this way. He *made* us to use lists!

The list hub

The best way to organize all of your various lists (and I have a lot of list ideas coming right up) is to keep them in your daily planner. By now, your planner should be centrally located, so you'll usually be close by when an idea strikes you. The only lists that shouldn't go in your planner are your shopping lists—you'll want to keep those out on your fridge where everyone in your family can add to them.

Technology Girls, yes, you can use your computer or smart phone to store your lists. Just remember what my momma says: it's not a matter of *if* your technology will die, it's *when*. Back everything up! And to keep everything together where it will never be lost or accidentally erased, give your planner a try. (You know I can't help it.)

Jesus Moms, get ready to complete your planner by filling in that tabbed section in the back! Most planners have these tabs, or a section dedicated to "notes," with plenty of blank pages on which to write. This is the perfect place for your fleeting thoughts to become organized lists. Hopefully, you already have your Goal List and Greater To-Do List back there.

If you have a ring-bound planner system, you can use the included tabs to indicate where you're keeping each list. The tabs in some planners are pre-printed with list ideas that may apply to your life at home or at work, but you'll need to add your own titles, as well. You can trim plain white labels down to cover the pre-printed tabs so you can customize the back section of your planner for the lists *you* want to keep.

Purge those pieces of paper (please)

When you're finished, you'll be able to flip right to the list you want whenever you need to consult it or add to it. No more searching through piles of paper, looking for the right one and hoping it didn't get blown under the refrigerator. In fact, after you've customized your planner and written your lists down in the back, there shouldn't be any "floater" pieces of paper in your work space at all. If your information can be lost or forgotten, it might as well be floating around in your mind!

Sometimes you'll have information on a piece of paper that you can't or don't want to re-write, like an invitation with an address on it. You don't have to get rid of the actual paper if you don't want to. You just need to make sure you've thought through what you need to do about the information it holds, and then put the piece of paper in the right place.

When you get a wedding invitation in the mail, the first thing you need to do is write the date on your Family Calendar. Before you forget, fill out the RSVP! Then make a note on your shopping list to buy the happy couple a wedding gift, and maybe even yourself a new dress. If you need to get a sitter for the wedding day, give her a call or write a reminder on an upcoming daily to-do list. If you need to travel for the wedding, or if you're a member of the bridal party, you'll have lots of other to-dos to write down.

Once you've thought through what that wedding invitation requires of you and you've written all of those things down, you can let it go. Now you can paper clip the invitation and driving directions to the page in your planner that corresponds with the actual day of the wedding. Or you can attach it to your Family Calendar (some calendars even have pockets for this purpose), where it will wait for you until you need it.

By taking a few moments to plan and prepare, you've set your mind and heart at rest about that wedding. You won't stumble across the invitation over the next few weeks and think annoying thoughts like, *Oh, right, I have to remember to get a sitter for that wedding,* or *What am I going to wear to that wedding?,* or worse, *Did I remember to RSVP?* You've taken care of business, your desk is clear, and so is your mind!

File it away

The vast majority of your thoughts and ideas can be contained and organized in your planner. If you aren't in the habit of making lists, you may not recognize how many of your fleeting thoughts can be written down in an organized way! So I'm going to give you some suggestions for lists you may want to keep in your planner.

Yes, I love lists so much that I'm giving you a list of possible lists. You may already have some of these lists floating around, some may appeal to you more than others, and of course you may think of more! I just want to get you thinking about the things that clutter up your mind—things that could be organized on paper in your planner, instead.

Some of these lists may thrill you so much that you won't want to cram all of your related ideas into your planner. You can create a file folder for your ideas and keep it under your planner or in your home office. You may even have a whole binder full of ideas related to one or more of these topics, or an overflowing Pinterest board (just be selective enough that the practical-for-you ideas don't get lost in a crowd of super-cute things you'll never really do).

You need to do what works for you. The important thing is that you're writing down your terrific yet fleeting thoughts, ideas, and inspirations—keeping track of the important things in your life. Read over my list ideas and decide which ones will clear the clutter out of your spirit so you can live in the Lord's peace. Who knows, soon your hubby may be calling *you* "List Lady." (I'd take it as a compliment!)

The Goal List and Greater To-Do List

We've already discussed your Goal List, the list of projects and other goals you're currently working on, and the Greater To-Do List, the list of things you want to do but don't need to work on right now. These will be your most important long-term lists and should be at the very front of your list section. With these at hand, you'll never lose sight of exactly what you want to spend your time doing—now, and twenty years from now.

The grocery list

You probably have a grocery list going right now, stuck to your fridge with a cute magnet, and that's just the way it should be! You grocery list shouldn't be in your planner, but out in the open where anyone who drinks the last of the orange juice can write on it. For more efficient grocery shopping, try writing your food items down in loose aisle groupings, much like you separate your to-do list into time chunks.

At our house, we write fruits, vegetables and breads near the top of the list, followed by canned goods. Baking goods and recipe ingredients are generally written in the middle. Frozen foods, meats, and dairy are at the bottom of the list so we'll pick up those keep-cold items last. Our grocery coupons are loosely organized by aisle in their accordion folder. With a loosely organized list, we can easily work our way through the store from one end to the other.

If you'd like to try grocery shopping only once a week, you should hang a separate meal planning list next to your grocery list. My beautifully organized sister-in-law, Kristen, assigns different meals to different days, with a leftover day at the end of the week, so she always knows exactly what she's going to make (seriously impressive). I'm more flexible about cooking—in other words, I hate to cook and avoid it as much as possible. If we have enough leftovers, I don't cook. If my husband calls and says he's not coming home for dinner, I don't cook. My Meal List can last me up to two weeks (impressive in a different way).

Once a week on Errand Day, choose the dishes you'd like to make and write them on your Meal List. Be sure to check your Family Calendar so you don't forget about snacks you've volunteered to bring somewhere, or dishes you want to make for guests. Also, check your pantry and fridge for things you have on hand that you need to use before they expire. Then consult your recipes to see what ingredients and family staples you need to purchase to complete your recipes.

And don't forget the milk, milk, milk! My hubby and kids can go through a lot of milk in a week. (I hate milk, except as a vehicle for lots and lots of chocolate syrup.) You'll probably need to buy multiples of your family's favorite staple foods, or you may need the same ingredient for two different recipes. If so, indicate the amount to be purchased, for example, "milk x3."

If you're like me, you'll waste less food this way. Checking my pantry before I go shopping keeps me from buying things I already have, and my Meal List reminds me to use what I bought. I have a tendency to look in the fridge and think things like, *Why on earth did I buy six green peppers?* My Meal List reminds me that I was planning to make stuffed peppers, that's why. (Yum!)

Once you're in the habit of planning your meals and writing well-thought out grocery lists, you'll be amazed at how easy grocery shopping becomes—once-a-week grocery shopping can be done, Jesus Moms! And when it's time to make dinner, instead of staring at the pantry and deliberating over what you want to make (and possibly surrendering to the urge to ask your husband to grab some take-out on the way home, again), you can just check your Meal List.

A general running shopping list

This is the list of non-grocery items you'd like to buy on your next Errand Day, and it's also best kept in plain sight on your refrigerator where your husband and kids can learn to write on it. When you think of something you'd like to purchase, write it on this list instead of running right out to get it. You'll save time and gasoline, you'll avoid impulse buys, and you may even decide you don't need that item after all.

Many individual items need to be purchased at separate stores, which is why this list can double as a list of Errand Day destinations. If there's a store you frequent for several items at a time, you may want to make an individual list for that store, just like your grocery list. In our house, we keep a running Target list for things like paper goods, pet supplies, and other household items.

If you have one or two favorite stores that deserve their own lists, hang those lists up on your refrigerator, too. Luckily, those are the last lists your fridge needs to hold! The lists from here on out go in the back section of your planner, because you'll be the only one writing on them.

A list of medical information

This is an important one, Jesus Moms. You should consider keeping an easily accessible record of medical information for each person in your home. Behind this tab in your planner, keep brief health histories including blood types, allergies, current medications, and social security numbers for you, your husband, and your kids.

Be sure to write down the names of the various doctors in your life with their phone numbers and addresses, as well as driving directions to their offices. Write down the address and hours of your closest urgent care facility as well. And, you can keep any insurance information you may need there.

I can't tell you how many times I've used this list to quickly access our pediatrician's and dentist's addresses for preschool forms and other emergency medical forms. Also, I love knowing exactly where to look when I need to write down Travis's social security number. (I do have it memorized, but it never looks right to me...probably because it's not mine.)

You can set your heart at ease by making all of this information easily accessible for yourself, your husband, and babysitters, too. Most of the time, you'll only need the information on this list when you're filling out boring paperwork—but if you do need your family's medical information in a stressful moment, then you'll have it right at your fingertips.

A list of homeowner information

This is another great list that can help to make stressful times a little less overwhelming. Even if your husband is really handy, you may find yourself needing the phone numbers of professionals such as plumbers, electricians, and appliance repairmen. When you find someone whom you trust to do good work in your home, record their information in this section of your planner. You can even staple their business cards right to the page.

This section of your planner is also the place to keep records of anything pertaining to your house, condo, or apartment. You can keep a list of different repairs or upgrades you've made. You may want to keep a record of décor-related items, like paint colors, room measurements, and window treatment measurements. You can also keep a record of your landscaping efforts here. (Without a little map of my flowerbeds, I've been known to accidentally weed my perennials in the spring.)

You can also use this space to plan a timeline and start a budget for any kind of home improvement or landscaping venture. Nurture your inner decorator and write down your design ideas, or attach pictures of home décor that you admire right to the page. (You creative, trendy girls may want a whole binder for this one!) This list is the perfect place for all of the information, plans, and dreams you have for your home.

A list of things borrowed or lent

Here's a list I'll admit I don't keep. I don't really like to borrow things, and I have an instinctual sense about things that don't actually belong in my house (I can spot a library book hiding on my kids' bookshelves a mile away). On the flip side, I tend to lend things with great abandon and then forget all about them. In fact, I'm usually surprised when people return an item to me because I either forgot I owned it or thought I still had it. I don't carry any spiritual clutter about things I've borrowed or lent...but you might.

The Bible has a lot to say about borrowing and lending. Like so much of the Biblical instruction about Christian living, it really comes down to how you treat other people. As Christians, we're supposed to lend freely, with an open heart, and yet not be indebted to others. Psalm 112 tells us that:

Good will come to him who is generous and lends freely,
who conducts his affairs with justice.

Psalm 112:5

Keeping a Borrowing and Lending List may help you to conduct your affairs with justice. If keeping track of the things you're lending allows you to soften your tight grip on your belongings, then this is the list for you. Or if you recognize about yourself that you're a forgetful borrower, then this list will keep you accountable. Make a monthly chore card or notes on a few Monthly Lists to remind yourself to check this list as often as you'd like. If you make and keep it with the right spirit, this list can help you to be an even better ambassador for Christ in the world.

A Special Days List

This running list of special days is a Jesus Mom "must" because it reminds you to shower a little extra love on your friends and family members when the time is right. You can keep your important dates, like birthdays, anniversaries, and holidays, written all together in one big, orderly list, starting with January 1st and ending with December 31st.

Each December, I spend a few minutes writing all of these special events onto the pages of our brand new Family Calendar. I even write the names of the holidays in my own handwriting because my eyes may fail to see those pre-printed holiday names among the myriad of handwritten activities. I missed a couple of Mother's Days that way when I was in college (sorry, Mom). I keep this list of important dates behind a marked tab in the back of my planner.

My planner also came with a section for addresses and phone numbers, but I don't use it. It makes my planner a little bulky, and I like having a separate address book stored along with stamps, return address labels, and greeting cards. If you decide to utilize the address book section in your planner, your Special Days List is a great list to keep right next to it.

Don't forget to add the new "special days" in your life to your list, like the anniversary of a newly married couple or the birthday of a new friend or new baby. If you keep a list like this and update it regularly, you'll never miss a special day again… and you'll intentionally share God's love with the ones you love.

A Gift Ideas List

Another way to show love to your family and friends is by giving gifts they'll actually enjoy. This is a very challenging area for me—try as I might, I'm not a very creative gift-giver. Sometimes lightning does strike and I think of a great gift idea. I'll be in a store, see an item, and think, *That looks just like so-and-so...* So I write the idea down on my Gift List. Even if I purchase the item, I make a note on this list so I don't forget that I bought it. (Ever do that? Yup, me too.)

More often, I cheat by writing down any little hints my loved ones give me about what they'd like to have. These hints are everywhere—if you're listening for them. When a friend comments on how pretty your necklace is, make a note on this list so you'll remember to look for something similar for her next birthday. Listen for comments like "This thing drives me crazy" or "I wish I had a new..." Write down those things that your husband and kids openly admire in stores, in sale ads, or at someone else's house. Make note of your loved ones' clothing sizes and favorite treats.

If you pay attention, you can make a really great Gift List. Write it all down so you don't forget and clutter up your spirit with *I know I had a great idea for her, what was it?* thoughts. Even if you're a great gift-giver, having a solid list of gift ideas can be very helpful—when Christmas rolls around, you'll be ready.

Your Christmas List

No, this isn't part of your gift list for others. Nor is it the wish list your child may be making for Santa. This is a wish list for *yourself*. And don't jump right to the conclusion that it's selfish or greedy to write a list like this.

Jesus Moms, of course we're allowed to want things! We just have to guard against the feelings of discontentment and dissatisfaction that can come with the wanting. Thoughts about the things you'd like to have can clutter up your spirit just like all of your other distracting thoughts—and just as before, writing these thoughts down helps clear the clutter out of your head and heart.

Keeping a list of wants can actually help you to be *more* satisfied with all that you have. When you're flipping through a magazine or looking around someone else's home, and you spy something you'd like to have, just write it down. You'll turn a discontented, *I really wish I had that* thought into a hopeful, *Well, maybe I'll have that someday* thought—and then you can stop thinking about it altogether. And sometimes you'll write something on your Christmas List only to find that by the time December rolls around, you don't really want it any more—*What was I thinking? I'm good without it.*

You can also curb impulse buying with your Christmas List. I remember going out shopping with my mom when I was little and giving her puppy-dog eyes when I saw something I desperately wanted. By cheerfully responding, "Well, put it on your Christmas List!" she taught me about delayed gratification at an early age. And Mom continues to be an example for me—starting December 26th, she still puts almost everything she wants on her Christmas List…and she's truly happy whether she gets these things or not.

Then, when my dad, brother, sister, and I are trying to think of gifts for her, she has a gift for us: a great list of ideas to help us along! If you let your husband know you're keeping this list in the back of your planner, he may really appreciate it—and not just at Christmastime! You can make things easier for your husband and kids on your birthday and Mother's Day by keeping a list of things you'd like to receive.

So really, this list isn't selfish at all—it's very utilitarian. In fact, the lists in this chapter have all been very effective and important ways to take care of our families and our homes. Each of these lists will keep your *I have to remember that* thoughts from weighing you down, so you can live with your heart lifted *up* to Jesus.

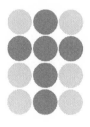

Chapter 9

Fun and Jesus Lists

So now that we've corralled your *I have to remember that* thoughts with some great utilitarian lists, let's tackle your *I want to remember that* thoughts with lists that are a little more fun! Lists aren't just for the "hum-drum" stuff of everyday life. They can help you enjoy your family and strengthen your relationships in real ways, even your most important relationship: your relationship with the Lord. We're going to take a look at all of the lists—from silly to spiritual—that will get the "I want to" clutter out of your spirit and into your organizational system.

Lists of books and movies and other fun

The lists behind these marked tabs in your planner are about the things you like to do for fun. If you keep a list of favorite authors and books you'd like to read, you'll be ready the next time you're looking for a book to take on vacation (because moms always have *tons* of time to read on family vacations). With a list of new restaurants you'd love to try, you can avoid the classic "Where do you want to eat?", "I don't know, where do *you* want to eat?" date night conversation.

Your hobbies can also inspire some great lists. One of my favorite hobbies is photography, so I have a list of photos I'd like to take some day. For example, when Oliver's a little older I want to take a picture of my three darlings showing off their belly buttons, and a picture of them jumping up in the air with their hair flying and air beneath their feet. Sometimes I cut cool pictures like these out of magazines and attach them to my list. With my photo ideas list, I'll remember to take these wonderful, creative pictures of my kids as they grow up.

With your fun lists, you can intentionally remember to follow up on the recommendations of friends and family members, letting them know that you value their opinions. And your fun lists are the perfect way to keep track of recommendations you've read on websites or blogs or pinned on Pinterest before you forget them. No matter what your sources, these lists will be uniquely *you*, ready to inspire you whenever you're ready to enjoy one of these small but wonderful blessings from God.

Lists of vacation, daytrip, and activity ideas

Newspapers, magazines, websites, blogs, and other moms are full of terrific ideas to help you have fun and enjoy your time with your kids. When you see or hear of something regarding a family vacation destination, outing, or activity your family would enjoy, write it down in this section of your planner. You can write down the actual ideas, jot down the web addresses, or attach any related article right to the list. (You may even want a binder for this one—God's given us so many fun things to enjoy!)

If you're interested in replicating a friend's vacation, even after you've seen all 350 photos of her trip, write the destination down on your vacation ideas list. If your family isn't quite ready for that much adventure, make sure to note the approximate year you think the vacation would be appropriate for your kids so it won't pass you by. You may also want to keep a list of romantic places you'd like to visit with your husband—even if you don't see any of these places until you're an empty nester.

If you're like me, you'll want to keep track of your ideas for daytrips or even shorter outings so you don't miss the wonderful opportunities right in your backyard. I learned this the hard way. Soon after we moved into our current abode, a friend told me that there's a chocolate factory (a *chocolate* factory) tucked away in an industrial area less than ten minutes from our home. Sadly, it took me a few years of *Oh, right, I should check that out* thoughts before I actually took my kids on the factory tour.

Well, it was awesome. Chocolate pouring out of tubes, and big vats of cream fillings, and free samples. I was overcome with delight and my taste buds sang. (I should mention that my kids thoroughly enjoyed watching the factory workers and seeing big machines making the chocolates, too.) I couldn't believe I'd waited so long! If only I'd been more intentional about going... Mmm, *more* chocolate.

There's so much fun to be had with the kids when we're home together, too! I have an entire binder filled with craft and activity ideas that I frequently force my kids to enjoy (they'll look back on it fondly someday, I just know it). If you're a little less gung-ho, a list of interesting at-home activities is a great thing to keep in your planner. And don't forget to add the fun activities you remember from your childhood so you can re-create them for your own kids.

I have wonderful memories of building tents made with sheets and clothespins in the Kelley family living room with my brother and sister. We'd color, and play board games, and listen to records under there. (Records... Wow, I feel old.) Shortly after Spencer was born, I bought some plastic clothespins specifically for tent building (at least I don't pre-date the clothes dryer) and swore never to let go of an old sheet. The kids and I have built some pretty deluxe tents together, and I love playing with them in there. It's way more fun to shout "Uno!" in a sheet tent—that's just a fact.

So when a fond childhood memory makes you smile, write it down in your planner so you'll remember to do something similar with your kids. Activities like these, possible daytrips, and vacation ideas are all great things to write down so you'll be intentional about doing them when your kids are the right age to enjoy them. These ideas can be especially great for moms and their kids during the summer months when everyone is out of school. You can use these lists to take your family on vacation from the everyday for a week, a day, or just an afternoon.

A "Kids Say the Darndest Things" List

Spencer started getting *Star Wars* fever around the time I potty trained him—not because I let him watch the movies, but because of the merchandising. And, of course, because his dad couldn't wait to pass on his love of all things George Lucas. One day soon after my little Jedi had mastered his new potty skills, he was sitting on the throne, doing his thing, and thinking. He gave me a serious, contemplative look, and said, "Mom, I bet when Chewbacca goes to the potty, he poops every time."

I howled with laughter and swore I would never forget my sweet little guy's innocent witticism. And I won't forget it, because I wrote it down. Each of my kids has a list in my planner of funny things they said or did. I love to read over those lists again and again, and the kids love to hear their stories over and over, as well. (Admittedly, Spencer may be less than pleased to read his infamous Chewbacca comment here...but it was so cute I had to share!)

One day last year, four-year-old Karly looked at me with total sincerity and said, "Mom, sometimes I think we're in a storybook, and I'm the Rockin' Star." That comment filled my heart with joy—isn't that just how childhood should be? Our children *are* Rockin' Stars, placed onto our families' center stage by our Creator. We want to remember the best lines of the show!

The funny or poignant things your kids say and do are gifts straight from God. They keep you going on the days when your little stinkers write with permanent markers on the walls. You can write their adorable moments on the tablet of your heart by jotting them down in your planner, never to be forgotten.

A list of people to see

Speaking of forgetting, you know you've done this: you're at your moms' group, and a new acquaintance says, "We'll have to get together some time…"

So you say, "Oh, right, we should. I'll call you…" and you both walk away, and you don't call her.

Sometimes you don't call her because you were just being nice and you don't want to get together some time. If so, shame on you. (Just kidding.) But, sometimes you really *do* want to get to know her better and you just forget all about it. Instead, use this list to write down the names of the women you'd like to spend time with. If you know their husbands' names or the names and ages of their kids, write them down for a quick refresher before a playdate. (I'm not the only one who can't remember these things, right?)

Then, the next time you feel like taking your kids to the zoo, or even just to the park, you can ask one of these women if they'd like to meet you there. If you're really gung-ho, you could invite her whole family over for an evening dessert, so the kids can play while the grown-ups get to know each other and savor some chocolate yum. Or be brave and go for the "come on over for dinner" evening right away. In any event, including the kids in the first get-together will give you a plausible excuse to leave if things are going south.

Making new friends is just like dating, isn't it? You have to be purposeful about getting yourself out there. This list might have you kissing a few frogs, but then God might be trying to give you the matchless blessing of a new friend, and you don't want to let that blessing slip away.

Keeping this list will also keep you open to the whisper of the Holy Spirit when he gently nudges you to care for someone. Like when you realize that a friend has been looking a bit down lately—maybe you should give her a call and see if she'd like to get together. Or your non-Christian friend seems more receptive to your faith-related comments lately—maybe it's time to get together and really talk about Jesus. Listen to these nudges and use your list to intentionally build these eternal relationships.

The list of people you want to see can also hold the names of old friends you haven't seen in a while. If you've dropped the ball in a game of phone tag, or if busy schedules are getting in the way, be intentional about reaching out. Try keeping this list of new friends, old friends, and non-Christians friends to refer to when you're ready for some company. [1] Pray over it as well, lifting up all of these special women to the Lord who brought you together.

---

1 If you need some fresh hostessing ideas, check out the "Party Hearty!" article on OrganizingJesusMoms.com.

A Prayer List

OK, you know you've done this, too: a friend says, "Please pray for me," and you say, "I will" and you both walk away, and then you forget to pray for her. You *always* mean this one and have the best of intentions, but sometimes you just forget.

If you have the opportunity, pray with the person right away. There's no time like the present and the Lord loves it when we come to Him in prayer together. But if you don't, write it down. You'll probably want to write it down even if you have already prayed with her! God wants us to pray continually in all circumstances, and keeping a Prayer List reminds us to do that. If you've never kept a prayer journal before, you'll be amazed to witness your requests turning into praises as the Lord answers your prayers in His own perfect way and timing.

There are probably some "big picture" topics you'd like to pray over as well, but forget about when life gets busy. These issues may include institutions or people and can be local, national, or global. I like to pray for my kids' teachers and our school system, our local and national government officials, doctors and researchers who work to heal, and pastors and missionaries who are doing the Lord's work worldwide. I keep a list of prayer topics in my Bible, and try to pray over one topic a day. This list keeps my heart focused outward, beyond the walls of my own home where my mind can become so focused.

Another powerful way to pray is to pray over scripture, letting God's own words express what you're feeling. When Travis is out of town on a business trip, especially when he's flying or I know he's in a big city, I like to pray Psalm 91 over him. It begins like this:

> He who dwells in the shelter of the Most High
> will rest in the shadow of the Almighty.
> I will say of the Lord, "He is my refuge and my fortress,
> my God, in whom I trust."
> Surely he will save you from the fowler's snare,
> and from the deadly pestilence.
> He will cover you with his feathers,
> and under his wings you will find refuge;
> His faithfulness will be your shield and rampart.
>
> *Psalm 91:1-4*

I sometimes use these very words to ask the Lord to protect Travis on his travels. More often, I read the psalm, and then use my own, parallel words to lift Travis up to the Lord. It's a little different every time, but I usually pray something like this:

> Oh Lord, Most High, please let Travis dwell in Your shelter
> and rest in Your shadow as he is away from us. Be his

refuge and his fortress, my Father God in whom I trust. Protect him from evil and sickness. Cover Travis with Your wings wherever he goes and help him to grow closer to You.

You are so faithful to us, Lord;

thank You for loving and protecting our family always.

Praying the psalmist's words over Travis, especially when I pull them into my heart and pour them back out to God in my own way, is incredibly comforting to me. You can write your own "go to" scriptures and prayers on your Prayer List.

A Scripture List

You may want to keep a separate list of scripture verses as well—verses God has used to touch your heart. Maybe you were reading your Bible at home when a verse just leapt off the page at you. Or you heard a scripture-based song on the radio that moved you, so you looked up the verse. Maybe the pastor read a verse during his sermon that gave you a light bulb moment. You can keep a list of these scripture references in your planner, or even better, write out the actual verses and what they mean to you.

Some of your spiritual "ah-ha" moments may not come directly from God's Word, but from the words of his servants on Earth: pastors, Christian authors, lyricists, and inspirational speakers. When your heart is touched by something you've read or heard, write it down so you can mull over and remember it.

You may also want to keep a list of scripture verses or faith-filled quotes for times when you're feeling different emotions. Specific verses can help you feel close to the Lord when you're afraid, anxious, weary, or even joyful. Write down the verses that make your heart sing when you want to praise Him, and the ones that lift your heart up to the Lord when you're in the depths.

I've already shared with you some of the verses that assuage my anxieties and calm my fears. I also have favorites that lift my heart to the Lord in joy or thanksgiving. Right next to my planner, I've posted the first verse of "Joyful, Joyful, We Adore Thee":

> Joyful, Joyful, we adore Thee,
> God of Glory, Lord of Love;
> Hearts unfold like flowers before Thee,
> Opening to the sun above.
> Melt the clouds of sin and sadness;
> Drive the doubt of dark away;
> Giver of immortal gladness,
> Fill us with the light of day!

When I cannot express the depth of my joy in the Lord, I turn to these words and shout them with my heart (or even sing them aloud). I also have scriptures I turn to when I'm feeling other emotions too deep for my own words. If you have scriptures that comfort you or clearly express your heart's cry to the Lord, then you can keep them in your planner, centrally located and right where you'll be able to find them when you need them.

A Blessings List

The tabbed section of your planner also is the perfect place for a list of blessings. Jesus Moms, our hearts are so thankful to the Lord for all kinds of things!

I went to a moms group recently where the women present were challenged to share something they were thankful for—but not just any old blessing. It had to be something they thought no one else in the world would be thankful for that day. I heard about a mom's thankfulness for a wobbly vase that didn't fall. Another mom told about her sons' extremely active nature and how it keeps her feeling energized. One mom shared about a Lego set that has brought together three generations of builders. (OK, the Lego Mom was me.)

Your list of blessings will be different from anyone else's. You'll gain joy from writing down all of your blessings, especially the "everyday" ones you might otherwise forget. And when you're having a down day, this list will be exactly what you need to keep your heart centered in Jesus.

A Most Wanted List

My parents' pastor gave me the idea for the "Most Wanted" list—a list of non-Christian family members and friends whose hearts you covet for the Kingdom of Heaven. Jesus Moms, helping others to come into a relationship with God is one of the deepest purposes of our lives here on Earth. (I'm no theologian, but I'll venture to say it's *the* deepest purpose.) God hears our prayers for loved ones who don't know Him, and may choose to answer us with opportunities to witness to them. And when you add your kids' names to this list, you'll be reminded to pray over their salvation regularly.

If keeping written lists of prayer requests, scriptures to pray over, blessings, and unsaved people for whom to pray seems strange or mechanical to you, you can journal about all of these things in a notebook or binder instead. My challenge to you is to write down the thoughts and ideas you want to share with God so you'll remember to lift them up to Him. You'll please His spirit with the offering of your own.

Remember that these spiritual lists and the fun other lists I've mentioned are not "musts." I'm not saying you have to have a beautifully organized planner and awesome lists to live a Christian life—but I am encouraging you to be intentional about enjoying your time with your family and growing in your relationship with

God. Whatever they may be, the lists you choose to keep will clear some of the clutter out of your spirit and be invaluable resources for you as you walk with the Lord in the months and years ahead.

Gathering your thoughts

OK, you're thinking. *I'm with you, lists are great. But how am I supposed to write these thoughts down when I actually think them?*

You're right. If you happen to have an epiphany when you're close to your planner, it's awesome. That's one of the most helpful things about your planner being centrally located in your kitchen or on your desk at work or wherever you spend the most time. Unfortunately, many of your list-worthy thoughts will come to you when you're away from your planner. But with a little fore-thought, you can be ready to de-clutter your mind even when your planner isn't handy.

When you're at home

You can start by identifying the places in your home where inspiration frequently strikes and choosing to keep notepads and pens there. One obvious place is next to your bed. We've all heard stories about people waking up from a deep sleep with fabulous ideas dancing in their heads. Writers and other creative people are always scribbling on bedside notepads, right?

I don't know about you, but the only thing that wakes me from a deep sleep is the voice of one of my children, and as I'm getting up the only thing I'm thinking is, *How soon can I get back into my bed?* My bedside notepad doesn't catch any epiphanies when my alarm goes off in the morning, either. I am not a morning person. Just ask anyone in my family.

I *am* a night person, though, so I do keep a notepad by my bed. Some nights my mind is racing with thoughts—things I want to do tomorrow or remember in the morning—and I have trouble settling down and falling asleep until I write them on my little notepad. I also have random thoughts and ideas while I'm getting ready in the morning; my husband will attest that I'll stop blow-drying my hair, write something down on my bedside notepad, and then go back to blow-drying without a word. (Sometimes I'm still so groggy that the ideas don't make much sense, but most of the time they do and I'm glad to have them written down.)

Try keeping a pen and paper in the rooms where you spend the most time on each floor of your home, especially those places where your mind ruminates. If you don't want to leave them out in plain sight, you can put them in a drawer or another out-of-the way location. Just make sure they're there to catch your thoughts, ideas, and Holy Spirit inspirations.

After you've written a note to yourself, tear off the sheet of paper and carry it with you until you get to your planner. If it's something you want to *do*, write it down on the appropriate daily to-do list. If it's something you want to *remember*, write it down in the list section of your planner.

It may sound a bit nerdy, but after a short time this will become a habit you'll love. You'll find that your brain has been stuck on the same thoughts for weeks, or even months! Use your organizational system to make that thought a new goal, a new to-do item, a new chore card, a new item for a Monthly List, or a new item on one of your personal lists. Let go of the ideas rolling around in your head and clear out that spiritual clutter!

When you're out and about

Lots of great ideas pop up when you're out and about, shopping or talking with friends. Fortunately, since you're a mom, you're practically guaranteed to have a purse or diaper bag with you at all times. You should carry a pen and small notepad wherever you go, ready to capture your thoughts. In fact, you may already have these things in your purse but not be using them to their full potential.

This is one of the rare times when technology (i.e. your cell phone) can be your friend, as well. You can use even the most basic cell phone to leave yourself a message at home. If your phone has a camera, you can use it to take pictures that will jog your memory later—potential gift ideas, Christmas list ideas, books you'd like to get from the library later, or movies you want to rent sometime. I suppose you could even sneak a picture of a friend you want to get to know, as long as you can do it without looking like a stalker.

The paper-lover in me has to put a damper on the technology love here, though. Once you get a text or voicemail or reminder or photo on your phone, it's easy to forget it's there. Your ideas are only good if they don't get lost or forgotten. Most of the time, the handy-dandy notepad in your purse works just as well if not better than your phone for giving yourself reminders.

If you write the idea down on an actual piece of paper, you can lay it on the car seat next to your purse, or put it in the bag with your purchases, or wrap it around your phone or your car keys or some other frequently used item. Anything, just as long as you'll be sure to see it when you get home and write it in the appropriate place in your organizational system.

Displacement

This paper habit is a kind of object displacement—moving an object to a place it shouldn't be to remind you of something. I think everyone does this occasionally, and it works well with a piece of written information. But often, moving random things around isn't very helpful. Like when you see your car keys on the dryer and think, *Wait, why did I put those there?* Then you're even *more* bothered, which is the exact opposite of what we're trying to accomplish here. If you're going to displace something as a reminder, choose an object that's related to your thought.

Earlier this week I successfully displaced dirty pjs to remind me to take some home movie footage of Oliver. Lately, he's been unable to fall asleep until he's wriggled one of his arms out of the sleeve of his shirt. When I go into his room to wake him up, there he is in his crib, grinning at me, with his shirt collar stretched under one of his armpits. It's adorable. *He's* adorable.

It's one of those things that, as a mom, you think you'll always remember…but know you might forget. So I decided to get it on video. Unfortunately, each time I went into Oliver's room and remembered my plan, it was too late. He had seen me and I couldn't leave the room to grab the camera without making him cry (which would make for far less cute footage). And by the time I finished a diaper change *and* a bedhead battle, I'd forget all about getting the camera for next time.

Finally, one morning I threw his dirty pjs down in the middle of his bedroom floor. Since Oliver is a baby, his bedroom floor is generally empty, so the dirty pjs were very noticeable. (Note: This would not have worked in Spencer or Karly's rooms.) When

I came back up to Ollie's room to tuck him in, I saw the pjs and grabbed the video camera, placing it right outside his bedroom door. Then, when Ollie woke up, I got some precious video of him beaming at me, waving his paci with one naked arm. Success!

If you can't seem to write something down, try some displacement—just make sure that what you're displacing will actually remind you of what you want to remember (*Pjs... Oliver with his arm out of them... Video camera!*). Little things like this are intentional ways that you can remember what needs to be remembered and do what needs to get done.

Jesus Moms, when your ideas, worries, to-dos, dates, records, desires, dreams, intentions, plans, thoughts, and even prayers are written down, your mind will be unbelievably clear to enjoy your family and focus on the Lord. No longer will your spiritual clutter separate you from the Lover of your soul. With your thoughts on paper, your heart will be that much more open to hear His voice and rest in His love.

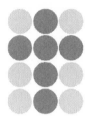

Chapter 10

An Uncluttered Spirit

Last chapter now, Jesus Moms. You've given thought to your ways and used organization to clear out your spiritual clutter about time, chores, activities, and ideas. That's some incredibly awesome work you've done. You've written down everything you need to in order to live your life intentionally.

There's just one kind of spiritual clutter left: the kind you should never, ever write down. In this chapter, we'll discuss how to gain control of your useless, hurtful, negative thoughts—thoughts that turn you into an Anxious Mom rather than the Jesus Mom you want to be. You'll learn to *demolish* your anxious thoughts. Does "demolish" sound a little strong to you? Check this out:

We demolish arguments and every pretension that sets
itself up against the knowledge of God, and we take captive
every thought to make it obedient to Christ.

II Corinthians 10:5

I mentioned in the first chapter that I suffered from a post-partum anxiety disorder after my second child, Karly, was born. During the first several months of this, I was a Certified Anxious Mom, times ten. It was an incredibly difficult time for me, but with a lot of prayer, scripture, and counseling, I began to learn how to deal with my consistently panicky thoughts.

Most of the anti-anxiety techniques I learned from the professionals in my life dealt with how to calm the *body*. I did find them to be helpful, especially when I combined them with prayer. Take deep breathing exercises, for example—rather than "breathing in the blue and breathing out the black," I called on the name of the Lord with each breath, Jeeeee (inhale) suuusss (exhale). When meditating, I didn't visualize lying in the sand on a quiet beach (which sounds hot and itchy anyway, am I right?); instead, I pictured myself lying in the palm of God's hand, often with my kids curled up beside me sleeping peacefully. My panic attacks became fewer and farther between, and I was increasingly able to live life on my terms.[1]

---

1 For more faith-based techniques to fight clinical anxiety (or just high anxiety moments), check out the "Reducing Anxiety with Jesus" article on OrganizingJesusMoms.com.

But then, through the second and third years of this affliction, I began to focus more on my *mind*. I started clearing out my deep-seated spiritual clutter and taking my anxious, lying thoughts captive. As God allowed me to struggle, I earned an honorary PhD in Recognizing Useless, Hurtful Thoughts and Kicking Them to the Curb. Imagine, if you will, Sensei Shannon karate-chopping numerous bad guys dressed in black. (Actually, it felt *a lot* like that.)

After four years of struggle, the Lord healed me and turned my clinical anxiety experience into a gift. I found that all of the anxiety-fighting skills I'd worked so hard to learn allowed me to dispatch of my "normal" anxious thoughts pretty quickly (hi-*ya!*). I'd learned that I have to be just as diligent about removing spiritual clutter as I am about keeping my home clutter free. And then the Holy Spirit gave me the desire to share what I've learned with you so that you could live life *abundantly*, growing even closer to Christ and shining like the woman of God and Jesus Mom that you truly are.

Taking control of your thoughts

Throughout this book, you've been learning how to organize *you*—how to feel organized on the inside. You know how to use your Daily Planning system, chore plan, and lists to really clear out your spiritual clutter. You're the Best Mom Ever now, right? You'll be able to do it all!

And you're thinking, *Ah, no.* "Doing it all" seems like something only those really-super-talented-at-everything women can do. I know a mom who's raising her little ones while she's running an outreach ministry. And she always looks *great*—she has a terrific sense of style to match her outgoing personality. One day I expressed my admiration of her to a friend, wondering aloud, "How does she *do* it all?"

My wise friend replied, "She doesn't!" And it's true. I don't know that she also cooks amazing, gourmet, organic meals. I don't know that she's teaching her kids a foreign language or three. I don't even know whether or not she has tons of laundry piled on her couch and toothpaste all over her sink. I shouldn't be admiring her for doing it *all*, I should be admiring her for doing what matters to her.

There's no such thing as "doing it all." In reality, there's only choosing what you really want to do and doing it well. I try diligently to do this, and mostly I succeed. (*But not all the time, Shannon. You could definitely do better*, my heart whispers as I type.) I know that there's no such thing as the Best Mom Ever, either, and I can't hold myself to that standard. (*But if there* was *a Best Mom Ever, it sure wouldn't be you,* says my heart. *No matter how organized you are, you really mess up sometimes.*)

Is your heart echoing mine? Do your thoughts chime in with "buts" whenever you try to let yourself off the hook a bit? These kinds of thoughts can be honest and true, borne out of humility. But, taken too far, they can be negative lies, bringing us down—and "getting organized" won't bring them into submission.

There are times when the act of writing down all of your to-dos and ideas still won't calm your spirit. Some days, as moms, our brains are positively steeped in thoughts that we aren't good enough. We worry that things could go wrong. We fret that we're wasting precious time. We worry that we're not [whatever] enough. We wonder if we should be doing this mom thing differently, better.

Worries. Anxieties. Fears. Thoughts that are baseless, or related to things out of our control. They distract us, slow us down, and attack our self-esteem. They can take the pleasure out of the moment, or the day. They keep us from being joyfully present with our families and distance us from God. Writing these thoughts into our organizational system would serve no purpose—but, Jesus Moms, we can still fight them.

There are tons of Bible verses about negative thoughts, thoughts filled with fear and worry and anxiety. It's a huge reoccurring theme throughout scripture—in the Old Testament:

So do not fear, for I am with you;

Do not be dismayed, for I am your God.

I will strengthen you and help you;

I will uphold you with my righteous right hand.

Isaiah 41:10

In the New Testament, straight from the lips of Jesus:

Look at the birds of the air; they do not sow or reap or store
away in barns, and yet your heavenly Father feeds them.
Are you not much more valuable than they?
Who of you by worrying can add a single hour to his life?

Matthew 6:26 & 27

And in the letters to the early Christians:

Do not be anxious about anything, but in everything, by
prayer and petition, with thanksgiving, present your requests to God. And the peace of God, which transcends all
understanding, will guard your hearts and your minds in
Christ Jesus.

Philippians 4:6

The Bible is filled with references to our human tendency toward fear and worry, and the message is always the same: don't do
it. Don't fear, don't worry, don't be anxious. But as moms, even

awesome Jesus Moms, this seems like an uphill battle. After all, don't we have a special worry named just for us?

Mom Guilt

When Spencer was four, he was playing at a friend's house and kneeled on a matchbox car. The cut was pretty short in length and he didn't seem too bothered by it, so I put a Band-Aid on it and let him keep playing. What I hadn't yet realized is that Spencer has an incredibly high pain threshold. That cut was *really* deep and I should've taken him to the doctor for stitches—but I didn't, and now he has a white, puckered scar on his knee. When I see that scar, the Mom Guilt kicks in. *I should have taken him to get stitches. Why didn't I take him to get stitches? I'm a bad mom.*

Now, I am not a bad mom. I'm a good mom, a *great* mom, a mom trying to live according to Christ's example. At the time, with the knowledge I had, I made a good decision. And that scar is meaningless in the grand scheme of things—Spencer even thinks it's a little cool. I know all of these things, but I still have to remind myself of them whenever I see that scar. I have to take those guilty thoughts captive and make them obedient to Christ. And I know I'm not alone.

Recently, I was hanging out with a group of Christian moms when one of them shared a bit of her spiritual clutter about a parenting choice she'd made. "You know," she said, "I guess it's Mom Guilt."

Immediately another mom chimed in. "Oh no," she declared, "I've *never* had Mom Guilt. Never had it, never will."

As soon as I heard the second mom's words (and tone), I quickly turned to the first mom to make sure she wasn't getting Mom Guilt about *having* Mom Guilt. I was ready to jump to her defense, but thankfully, she seemed fine. The next thing I did was take a longer, deeper look at the second mom. *Is she serious? She's* never *felt guilt as a mom? Is that possible? Hmmmm. Sorry, Friend, but I don't think I believe you.*

Every mom has had some Mom Guilt. We all second guess ourselves and wonder if we're doing the right thing. We worry about how our choices are affecting our kids. Those thoughts are natural, but not acceptable. Actually, I hope that's what that second mom was really getting at: *I won't tolerate Mom Guilt. I've never let it bother me, and I'm not going to start now.*

Neither should we, Jesus Moms. Jesus doesn't want us to feel guilty about our prayerfully made parenting choices. When we love Him and seek to follow His call, He brings about good for our families no matter what we decide. And that's a promise:

And we know that in all things God works for the good of those who love him, who have been called according to his purpose.

-Romans 8:28

The only eternally significant parenting choice we can make is the decision to raise our children in the Christian faith. We Jesus Moms choose every day, over and over, to raise our children to know and love God. God has given us wonderful, resilient kids who can grow up knowing Him no matter where they go to pre-school, or how many extracurricular activities they're in, or where they end up getting into college.

This is Truth, and it demolishes our Mom Guilt. In fact, when we hold our anxious thoughts up against the knowledge of God, His Truth triumphs over all of our unfounded fears and worries and anxieties.

Letting the Truth set us free

Recently my friend Elizabeth told me one of her internal struggles about working full time. During the time she stayed home with her kids, she took them to the library at least once a week to enjoy library programs and check out books. Now, even though she feels good about her decision to return to work, her spirit is cluttered with dissatisfaction and guilt that their library visits are less frequent.

If Elizabeth gives some thought to her ways and decides weekly library trips are still important to her, she can use organization as a tool to make them happen. She could declare a weekly

"Library Day" and head there every Wednesday after school. Or she could arrange with another mom to rotate Saturday morning library visits so one mom takes all of the kids while the other one does a little cleaning. Or something else.

Basically, she could clear that clutter out of her heart by living with intention. That's what this whole book has been about. Many anxious, guilt-ridden thoughts are actually healthy and productive, pushing us to take action so we'll live our best lives for Jesus.

But sometimes we don't need to take action. I think that in her heart of hearts, Elizabeth is really OK with her choice not to take the kids to the library so often. She knows that her kids visit the library at school and are read to by their teachers every day. She mentioned that many moms don't even have weekly library visits on their radar. Deep down, she knows the truth: no action is required here—and no guilt, either.

Like Elizabeth, we can feel guilty about the choices we're making, even when we're convinced that they're the right decisions for us. Sometimes these guilty thoughts creep up when we hear about other moms who've made different decisions. Sometimes they're cries for reassurance from our husbands, friends, and family members. Sometimes they're just attacks by Satan. He loves Mom Guilt.

I don't spend too much time thinking about Satan, but I

know that he exists and wants to bring us down. Jesus Moms do incredibly important work for the Kingdom of Heaven, and he doesn't like it. "Bad mom" thoughts are just what our enemy likes to hear. He smiles when we feel guilty about our wise choices. He chuckles when we unfairly compare ourselves to other moms and find ourselves wanting. So Jesus Moms, let's not give him the satisfaction.

When we stumble over the spiritual clutter of one of those guilty thoughts, we need to hold it up against God's Truth. If the thought fails to stand in the light of God's Word and His calling in your life, then ask the Lord to take the anxiety from you. Close your eyes, place those worries in your hands, and lift your palms to Heaven. Decide to give those feelings to your Creator who loves you unconditionally. Surrender your spiritual clutter to God, and be redeemed by His Truth:

> Into your hands I commit my spirit;
> Redeem me, O Lord, the God of truth.
>
> *Psalm 31:5*

Instead of thinking in a downward spiral: *I miss taking the kids to the library... Maybe I should still be doing that... Sometimes I feel like I don't have enough time for the kids any more... Maybe I shouldn't be working*, we should ask our God of Truth to capture those thoughts and redeem them: *I miss taking the kids to the library... Oh Lord, please help me not to feel guilty about that... We really enjoyed our times there and I did a great job preparing them for school... Now they're ready to become lifetime readers, and I was a big part of that.*

There is a deeper, Godly truth about this kind of guilt-ridden spiritual clutter. That's what we should seek and choose to dwell upon. When wrong thoughts start to take us down, we can choose to look *up* toward our Heavenly Father and be redeemed by His truth.

The best defense is a good offense
(I know that's a sports thing, but it applies)

We can take this a step further in order to guard our hearts and minds in Christ Jesus. We can use the Truth to take proactive, preventative measures—thought shots that inoculate us against the evil one. And I'm not just talking about Mom Guilt, either. I mean *all kinds* of negative thoughts and fears and worries that are completely useless, or worse, hurtful to us.

When my postpartum year ended and my anxiety disorder was as strong as ever, I began to accept that I would have to battle my unbelievably terrible thoughts over and over again. Not coincidentally, right around that time, I was trying to figure out what to give up for Lent. (If you haven't heard of this, for some Christians it's a tradition to fast from something during the weeks before Easter in order to remember Jesus' sacrifice and draw closer to Him.)

Usually I gave up a favorite food item (chocolate!), but this time I was too afraid of choking to enjoy eating anything anyway. Sometimes I sacrificed my time by adding an activity instead, like volunteer work or a Lenten Bible study, but that was no good this time either—it was a struggle for me to leave the house just to get the mail.

Then I remembered something my dad had once given up for Lent: worrying. He chose a Lenten season when my brother, sister, and I all had big things going on in our lives. Normally, he would've been worried about each of us. Instead, every time he started to worry, he turned it into a prayer and gave his worry to Jesus. I was so proud of him.

In the depths of my anxiety, I decided to give up worrying for Lent as well—and not just worry, but all kinds of negative thoughts that were plaguing me. A little saying occurred to me (perhaps a Holy Spirit gift), and I made it into a mantra of sorts. I printed it out on little slips of paper and put them everywhere. I taped one on my bathroom mirror, placed one in my planner, hung one by the phone, and even put one in my coat pocket with my car keys. The papers said:

No worries—What's my hurry?—Who says I have to?

Can you hear the sing-song version in your head? *No worries, what's my hurry, who says I have to!* I could hear it in my head—and I heard it out loud every time my husband teased me about it. It is pretty silly, but these three phrases helped me so much that I've held them in my heart far, far past that Lenten season.

The hardest part back then was the first phrase. Just like my dad, I had decided to have *no worries*. So I attacked every worry with prayer and tried my best to let it go. This is no small feat for someone with an anxiety disorder, and even now, I have to be intentional about this. I try to surrender all of my worries to the Lord who loves me.

I also tried my best to eradicate the feeling that time was running out, that hurry-hurry-rush-rush feeling I think all moms get from time to time. I had it almost incessantly in those days, so I would stop to think, *OK, what's my hurry?* If Spencer is late to preschool, what will happen? Essentially nothing. If church runs long and Karly's nap is late, what will happen? Nothing again. If Karly wakes up before I have all the bathrooms cleaned, what will happen? *Nothing.* I took deep breaths and tried to s-l-o-w d-o-w-n.

The third part of my phrase had, and continues to have, the greatest impact on me. When I felt pressure to do things I was petrified to do, things I knew that the Best Mom Ever (and lots of my real, non-anxiety-ridden mom friends) would certainly do, I'd stop and think, *Who says I have to?*

One day a couple of months ago when I dropped off Karly at preschool, there was a sign-up sheet posted outside the classroom door. Her teachers were asking for sugar cookies, cans of frosting, and sprinkles for a class party the next preschool day. I sighed when I saw that sign, and not just because the snack was so unhealthy. I'd just been to the store the night before and didn't relish the thought of heading back. And Oliver and I had colds, so I definitely didn't feel like baking. These thoughts flew through my head while I reached out to pick up the pen so I could write my name in one of the blanks.

Then I stopped and thought, *Who says I have to?* There were twenty kids in Karly's class, and only six slots for parents to sign up. I'd just brought a treat for their last party, and I knew I could bring another one later in the year. I wasn't shirking my duty, or being lazy. I just didn't have to. *I'm still a good mom even if I don't do this.*

That's what "who says I have to" really means to me. *I'm a good mom, even if* I don't play Spencer's favorite games with him (trading card games made up solely for merchandising purposes, like Pokémon), and make him learn to play Parcheesi with me instead. *I'm a good mom even if* I don't have Karly in a sport as well as ballet—I know I'd rather have her playing at home than booked up with activities. *I'm a good mom, even if* I'm not a patient, sensitive potty-trainer, and I someday subject Oliver to the same potty-training boot camp that I forced on the older two.

As long as I'm meeting God's standards for living and mothering, *I* get to decide what my standards are from there. I can be a force against the busy, against the frazzle, against the *extra* in my life. When I think, *Who says I have to?,* I'm choosing to ignore the "shoulds." I'm deciding that what I think is best for me and my family is just fine.

My Lenten experiment ended up changing my thought pattern and bringing my heart closer to Jesus in a way I didn't anticipate. After a few months of repeating my little mantra, my defense became my offense. Now, when negative thoughts attack, I attack them right back. They can't even get a good foothold before I am shoving them out with an *I will not worry!* or an *I will not hurry through life!* or an *I will not feel guilty about that!* These kinds of positive thoughts are nearly automatic responses to the negative thoughts that repeatedly want to clutter up my spirit. They help to guard my heart and mind in Christ Jesus.[2]

---

2 For more examples of these positive thought responses to common spiritual clutter, check out the "Thought Shots" posts on OrganizingJesusMoms.com.

Happy thoughts

Now, as my husband will tell you, I'm still prone to anxiety—all moms are. We start to worry. We mull over problems that need to be solved. Indeed, we should ponder our negative thoughts to see if they ring true and need to be addressed. But if we deem a thought useless or hurtful, we can refuse to accept it, denying it space in our heads and our hearts. Out—or *up*—it goes.

Only you know what insecurity-driven thoughts circle around in your head. If you take a week or two to really listen, you'll hear your own worries and doubts about the kind of mom you are loud and clear. You may even be able to discern a pattern, or recognize thoughts that are keeping you from your goals. Once you know where Satan attacks your spirit, you can decide how you want to defend your heart from him.

With some prayer and self-reflection, you can intentionally shore up your spirit against these thoughts. You can try my little mantra out, or come up with your own positive phrases to repeat. You may come up with questions you can ask yourself to challenge those thoughts, or scriptures that speak truth into your life. Whatever aids and Truths you discover, drag them into the light— write them, frame them, print them, post them, and pray them. Decide to dwell on things that are true, noble, and right, as Paul instructed the Philippians:

Finally, brothers, whatever is true, whatever is noble,
whatever is right, whatever is pure,
whatever is lovely, whatever is admirable
—if anything is excellent or praiseworthy—
think about such things.

Philippians 4:8

We can choose to protect our spirits from wrong thinking by dwelling on these things, by remembering we are giving glory to Christ with our very lives. We are Jesus Moms, admirable and lovely, and the work we're doing for the Lord and our families is excellent and praiseworthy. We're entrusting the Lord with our hearts.

When we strive to keep our everyday thoughts obedient to Christ, that's when we choose to live in His abundance. We know we don't have to be brought down with our worries, because the Lord can take the weight. We don't have to feel like we're scurrying around, because God has given us the time we need. We don't have to hold ourselves to society's ridiculously high standard of the "perfect" mom, because our true goal is to please our Savior Jesus and our Father God. We choose to live in God's perfect peace:

You will keep in perfect peace him whose mind is steadfast,

because he trusts in you.

Isaiah 26:3

When we trust in our Lord and make our minds steadfast, He will keep us in perfect peace. By definition, you as a Jesus Mom trust that our Lord Jesus is on the throne! And throughout this book, you've been learning how to make your mind *steadfast*. You've learned to live with intention by channeling your true thoughts and worthy ideas into your organizational systems. And in this chapter, you've discovered how to tackle your negative, lying thoughts head-on with prayer and right thinking.

Jesus Moms, *that* is how you've organized *you* on this journey with Jesus. You've cleared out your spiritual clutter and made room for God's great gifts of peace, love, joy, goodness, and grace. Now, live life abundantly, with a full heart and a spirit free to enjoy your family and your Lord!

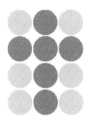

Afterword

Now that I've reached the end of this book, I have a confession to make: I am not a writer.

Yes, you are, you're thinking. *I happen to know this because I just read your book.* Well, much to my surprise, you've got me there.

What I really mean is, I don't enjoy writing. I'm a Math Girl. Any task that involves writing more than a paragraph is, for me, a true chore worth planning for—a chore that requires a happy uh-*huh!* check mark or a satisfying chore card *click!* upon its completion. I would much rather just tell someone what I'm thinking over a yummy cup of hot chocolate. I *love* to talk.

A few months ago, my local Mothers of Preschoolers group

asked me to come and speak about organization, and I jumped at the chance. For some reason, the Lord has gifted me with a love of public speaking. I happily chatted away at my MOPs friends for thirty minutes (well, maybe it was thirty-five…or forty), and then answered their questions about organization for the next quarter of an hour. It felt *wonderful.* (I didn't know it at the time, but that was the start of my speaking ministry.)

Later that evening, I told Travis all about my great experience. My super-supportive husband replied, "You should write a book!" I laughed out loud, went to bed, and forgot all about it.

Well, until about a week later. I was busy dusting away on Cleaning Day when I clearly heard a voice in my heart—*write the book.* And I couldn't shake it. Three days later I spent about a half an hour online reading about how difficult and time-consuming it is to write, and how, even if you're passionate about writing, it's almost impossible to get published. Well, I certainly wasn't passionate about writing. What was I doing even checking it out? Me, write a book? No, thank you.

In my heart, I pulled a Jonah and set sail for Tarshish—but the Holy Spirit was rocking my boat. I kept feeling the nudge deep down in my heart, *write the book.* I felt the Holy Spirit leading me in a clear, persistent way. God "nudged" me so hard I could practically feel it, and put "coincidences" in my path that were harder to ignore than a burning bush.

Actually, I started praying about writing this book much like Moses tried to get out of his assigned public speaking tour in Egypt—*Lord, who am I that I should write this? Why would women want to read what I've written? And I don't like to write. I have to work so hard at it, and it takes me forever. And my life is so full right now. Can't this wait until Baby Oliver is in school?*

I prayed and avoided, prayed and made excuses, prayed and made suggestions. Then I prayed and started listening. All I could hear was, *The time is now. Just start. I will help you.* So I decided to buckle down and get writing.

I immediately realized that I had no idea how to write a book. Instead, I pretended that you were a member of my moms' group audience, listening to me speak about your time, your chores, your thoughts, your family, and your life. The Lord put so much on my heart to tell you.

And I prayed some more. Lots more. And not just for the words, either. I prayed for *you*.

As you've been reading, you have been utterly covered in prayer. I prayed for *you*, my sister in Christ, every time I sat down to write. I prayed that God, my Father, would let me know what you needed to hear. I prayed that Jesus would sit beside me, leading me as I typed, reminding me of you with every paragraph. And I prayed that the Holy Spirit would fill me with words that would bring you help and hope.

My prayer for you now is that you'll take from this book everything you can in order to bring yourself closer to your loved ones and to God. My fervent desire is for you to wisely build your house by giving thought to your ways. My hope for you is that you become the Jesus Mom you feel called to be, the mom God made you to be.

Jesus Mom, you are the Lord's gift to your husband and your children. You are the woman He chose to take care of your family, a family that's even more precious to Him than it is to you. You are bringing glory to Christ each and every day, and He is so proud of you for the wonderful work you're doing. Enjoy each of His blessings, and every moment He has so graciously given to you.

Blessings to you, Jesus Mom,
Shannon

Now may the Lord of peace himself
give you peace at all times and in every way.
The Lord be with all of you.

II Thessalonians 3:16

About the Author
Shannon Upton

Shannon Upton is a Christian speaker, writer, and mom living in Central Ohio. Her books, talks, blog, and website are all devoted to helping her sisters in Christ clear the clutter out of their schedules, homes, and spirits.

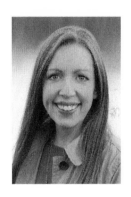

You can stay in touch with Shannon in several ways. For continued Jesus Mom encouragement, check out:

OrganizingJesusMoms.com
Facebook.com/Organizing*You*Ministries
Pinterest.com/ShannonKay4J
Twitter.com/ ShannonKay4J

If you have any further questions, or if you'd like Shannon to speak at your church or women's event, please feel free to e-mail her directly at shannon@organizingjesusmoms.com.

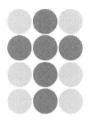

Study Guide

Steps along the Journey

Jesus Moms, I hope I've been clear that you have to organize in your own way, taking what I've written and making it work for *you* and *your family*—that's the only way you'll clear out your spiritual clutter! But, if you'd like to know exactly what steps I'd recommend for you as you take this journey with Jesus, here they are.

Chapter 1

1. Read the chapter and highlight anything that strikes your heart.
2. Pray over these reflection questions and spend some time writing out the answers to each of them:

- What clutters your spirit? Do you often feel hassled, hurried, inadequate or generally unorganized? How would you like to feel as you move through a typical day?

- How do you think your husband and kids view your household? Is your home a fun, relaxed place in which to live? What kind of atmosphere would you like to cultivate in your home?

- How do you want your kids to remember growing up in your home? How do you want them to remember you as a mother?

- Do you often compare yourself to other moms? Are the comparisons fair? Do you try to learn from other moms?

- What does the Jesus Mom look like to you? How are you like her now? What are some strengths you can celebrate and build upon? What are the "challenge areas" you'd like to improve?

- Do you struggle with God over control in your life? How can you focus on doing your best, and at the same time give your life and family to Him?

3. Review the highlighted sections and your answers, then make a short list of things you'd like to get from this book.

4. Look at your calendar and schedule the time you need to complete this book—maybe early mornings for the next nine days, maybe nightly after the kids go to bed, maybe

a long Saturday at a coffee shop (your husband will thank you in the end).

5. Set up rewards for yourself, or get an accountability partner. Pray about leading a group of women through a six-session study of the book—what a fabulous way to keep yourself accountable! (To make it really easy, e-mail me for a free Group Study Guide PDF through OrganizingJesusMoms. com.) Be intentional about finishing and working hard along the way!

Chapter 2

1. Read the chapter and highlight anything that strikes your heart.

2. Pray over these reflection questions and spend some time writing out the answers to each of them:

- Do you feel overwhelmed with things to do? Are you often running late or just running around? Does your level of "busy" affect your family? How would you like to feel?

- Are you ready to try a daily planner to better organize your time? If not, what's holding you back from taking this step?

- How can you strengthen each of your relationships with

friends and loved ones?

- How can you further the Kingdom of Heaven by culti-vating your relationships with non-believers?

- What kind of mother and woman of God do you want to be? Can you turn any of your negative thoughts about yourself into goals instead?

- Do some of your goals need to wait until a more appro-priate time? Which goals do you want to move to your Greater To-Do List?

- Which goals do you want to start tackling right now?

3. Review the things you highlighted as you were reading.

4. Prayerfully write your Goal List. Start with a brainstorm, then use the chapter as a guide as you consider your rela-tionships and personal goals.

5. Prayerfully consider your Goal List and pull out the things that can and should wait. Is this something God wants you to tackle right now? Will working toward this goal now negatively affect your family or your peace? Or is God call-ing you to get out of your comfort zone? Read the "Now and Later: Goal Setting" article on OrganizingJesusMoms. com and pray over those questions as well.

6. Star the goals that are chore-related and set them aside until you've read Chapter 4.

7. Sit with your Goal List and Greater To-Do List for a mo-

ment. Is God filling your heart with peace about the decisions you've made, or is the Holy Spirit bringing something to your attention? Don't move on until you feel completely at peace about your list.

Chapter 3

1. Read the chapter and highlight anything that strikes your heart.

2. Pray over these reflection questions and spend some time writing out the answers to each of them:

   - What's the first step for each of the goals on your list? When are you planning to take them?

   - Do you have a Family Calendar located in the best place for your family? How can you encourage your family members to use it wisely?

   - Is your day naturally divided into chunks of time? What kinds of tasks would be easiest for you to do in the morning, afternoon, or evening?

   - Do the things you *want* to do get buried under the things you feel you *have* to do? Do you tend to do fun or quick things before important things? Would prioritizing your tasks each day help you?

   - Do you tend to procrastinate? What are a few goals

you've put off even though they're really important to you? Do you need to set up a reward system or choose an accountability partner?

- What are some "busywork" tasks you could do during phone calls, while your kids are playing independently, or while you're watching a favorite TV show?

- Do you get distracted and leave things unfinished? When should you write a task down, and when should you just get it done?

- Do you turn to God in times of frustration? Do you have a favorite song or Bible verse that clears away your mental clutter and refreshes your spirit? How can you keep them at the forefront of your mind? (Maybe write them on the cover of your planner, or print them out and hang them next to your calendar.)

3. Now's the time to buy or make a daily planner. (Don't forget those free printable Organizing *You* planner pages on OrganizingJesusMoms.com!) Place your Goal List and Greater To-Do List in the list section in the back of the planner.

4. Purchase a Family Calendar if you don't have one (the ones with pockets are great).

5. Decide where to keep your daily planner and calendar so they'll be easy to access.

6. Decide on your natural "time chunks" and what kinds of tasks you do best during each one.

7. Prayerfully consider each goal on your list and choose the first step for each. Write that first step on the appropriate daily planner to-do list (or on your Family Calendar if it's a time sensitive task).

8. Decide how you'd like to use the memo space in your planner, if at all.

9. Choose a time of day (either late at night or early in the morning) to plan for the upcoming day and prayerfully dedicate it to the Lord. Use Appendix A to guide your Daily Planning time for the first few weeks.

10. Choose a scripture verse or song on which to meditate when your day doesn't go as planned. Write it on the cover or the front page of your planner. You may also want to print out a nice copy on your computer, frame it, and place it near your planner and calendar.

11. Review the sections you've highlighted and your answers to the reflection questions. Is there anything else you need to do before you move on?

Chapter 4

1. Read the chapter and highlight anything that strikes

your heart.

2. Pray over these reflection questions and spend some time writing out the answers to each of them:

- Do you have spiritual clutter about chores? How much do you think about your "should do's" on a daily basis?

- What's your current system for your big chores, and how's it working for you? Is there some room for improvement?

- Do you complete unpleasant tasks with a negative, "I have to" spirit? What are some of the "get to" benefits of your least favorite tasks?

- What chores do you *want* to do, and how often do you really *need* to do them? What's the bare minimum chore amount that will still leave you feeling fully satisfied?

- Do you want to try out the chore card system, or do you have a more technological version you'd like to try? (Don't worry, you won't hurt my feelings.)

- What daily chores do you tend to forget or put off? How do you feel when those things go undone? How can you be intentional about those chores?

- Does the usual level of clutter or mess bother any of your family members? How often should you do a quick pick-up?

- Take a look at your Goal List. Which goals can you start

reaching by assigning yourself daily tasks?

- Which chores seem never-ending to you? Can you imagine feeling "finished" with them? Are you open to scheduling "chore days"? Why or why not?

3. Purchase an index card box, white and colored index cards, and adhesive tabs if needed. Make sections in the box labeled "Daily," "Monday," "Tuesday," "Wednesday," "Thursday," "Friday," "Monthly," and "Monthly Lists." Cut a few cards of each color into three or four strips each.

4. Prayerfully make a list of daily tasks that you forget about or dislike. Think through your day—what things bother you because you don't get them done? Check Appendix D for additional ideas, but only include them if you really need the reminder.

5. Review your current Goal List, especially the chore-related goals you starred. Are there things you'd like to do every day with intention in order to reach one or more of those goals?

6. Review the sections you've highlighted and your answers to the reflection questions. Finalize your daily chore list.

7. Write your daily tasks on white chore cards and place them in the "Daily" section of your chore box.

8. Start laying out the daily cards next to your planner as you spend time preparing for the day ahead. They should be in a

neat column separated by time chunks, like a second to-do list. (See Appendix C for a visual.)

9. Try this system for a week or so. Is there anything you'd like to add or remove? Are there cards that you'd like to "demote" to once or twice a week? Tweak your daily cards so they're working for you…not the other way around!

10. Pray about the idea of "big chore days." Are you open to this idea? Why or why not?

Chapter 5

1. Read the chapter and highlight anything that strikes your heart.

2. Pray over these reflection questions and spend some time writing out the answers to each of them:

   - What five "big ticket" chores can you allocate to different weekdays, and forget about for the rest of the week?

   - How clean does your house need to be in order to satisfy your heart? How often do you need to complete your different cleaning chores? Or do your laundry?

   - Do you run a lot of unnecessary errands, or waste gas with inefficient routes? How can you consolidate your errands?

   - Do you make communicating with your friends and

loved ones a priority? Do you have any communication-related goals that lend themselves to chore card tasks?

- How much time do you spend online each day? Is this an area where the Holy Spirit is nudging you to consider changing your ways? What's the minimum amount of time you can spend with different technologies each day?

- Do you really enjoy your free time activities? Are their some less enjoyable free time activities you need to cut out in order to do the things that fill you up?

- Are you willing to schedule time for yourself to work on projects and enjoy hobbies? How do you think you would feel at the end of a Project Day?

- What are weekends like at your house? Do you relax and enjoy your family, or are you always trying to "get things done"?

- Do Sundays in your home have a special feel? What does a day of rest mean to you?

- If you're a working mom, or if your family has a non-traditional schedule, how will chore organization help you?

3. Prayerfully choose your chore days. Try taking a piece of paper and dividing it into six sections (one for each day but Sunday) with notes at the top about your daily com-

mitments (work on Tuesdays and Thursdays, preschool on Mondays and Wednesdays, etc.) so you can really see what your typical week looks like. Then assign chores to different days until they feel right.

4. Review your Goal List, highlighted sections, and reflection question answers. Finalize your weekly chore list.

5. Write your weekly tasks on the colored chore cards, using a different color for each weekday (possibly including Saturday), and place them in your chore box.

6. Consider your Sundays…how can you set them apart for the Lord? How will your family know that Sunday isn't just another Saturday? If there are chores you typically do on Sundays, try to allocate those chores to another day.

7. Start laying out your days-of-the-week cards with your daily cards in time chunks next to your planner. After a few weeks, assess your progress. Is there anything you'd like to add or remove? Are there cards that you'd like to "demote" to once or twice a month? Make sure your cards are clearing out your spiritual clutter and not adding to it.

Chapter 6

1. Read the chapter and highlight anything that strikes your heart.

2. Pray over these reflection questions and spend some time writing out the answers to each of them:

- What are some chores you only want to do once a month? What cleaning, laundry, errand-running, and communication-related chores can you do once a month (or even less)?

- How often would you like to plan dates for you and your husband? How often would you like to spend individual quality time with your kids?

- What are some ways you want to take care of yourself? What are some ways you could treat yourself once a month?

- What are some even less frequent tasks that you forget or dislike? What do you want to remind yourself to do once every few months, or once a year?

- What are some "spring" cleaning or seasonal mainte-nance chores you should do once or twice a year?

- How do you handle the chores involved in clothing your family? Is your spirit cluttered with negative thoughts about how "presentable" your kids are, or about the out-fits you're wearing? What realistic steps can you take in order to satisfy your heart about your own outward appearance?

- How are you at looking after your own health needs? Is

this an area where you need to encourage your husband as well?

- How can you make your home safer for your family? How do you want to handle safety issues like fire drills and stranger danger with your kids?

- Do you have a scripture to turn to when you worry about safety or other issues?

3. Pray over your Goal List and each of your big chore days and ask the Lord to reveal your monthly chores. Listen especially for anything that will help you grow closer to Him. Write a list of monthly chores.

4. Review the sections you highlighted and your answers to the reflection questions, then write your monthly chore cards on index card strips. Write and circle a capital "M" on these cards to set them apart.

5. Write the months of the year at the top of twelve index cards. Before you start writing your Monthly Lists, make sample lists on regular paper. Write the seasonal tasks first and consider your family's busy seasons, then fill in the other tasks on your lighter months. (Be sure to read all of Chapter 7 before you start to write on the actual cards!)

Chapter 7

1. Read the chapter and highlight anything that strikes your heart.

2. Pray over these reflection questions and spend some time writing out the answers to each of them:

    *   Do the tasks related to events, holidays, and other family fun often become chores for you? How can you be more prepared for the upcoming events on your Family Calendar?

    *   Do you sometimes worry that the time with your kids at home is flying by too quickly...and you might be missing it? How can you be more intentional about enjoying your time with your kids?

    *   How does your family celebrate holidays? How can you plan ahead to make your holidays less stressful?

    *   Are there any holiday or birthday traditions you'd like to start? Are there any family traditions from your husband's childhood that he'd enjoy continuing in your home? How can you make the Lord the focus of each holiday?

    *   How do you enjoy celebrating your husband and kids on their birthdays? Do you prepare enough so you can enjoy being with them on their big days?

- Do you have too many toys in your home? How do your kids view their toys? How can you foster a spirit of giving in them?

- Are you the family historian in your home? What does that mean to you? What related tasks would you like to accomplish?

- What ideas can you take from the last few chapters on time management and chore planning? How can you apply them to your life? How can you work toward your goals as a mother and woman of God?

3. As you review the last two chapters' highlighted sections and reflection question answers, continue to prayerfully add tasks to your sample lists. The seasonal tasks should stay put, but you can move around the non-seasonal tasks until the months are pretty balanced.

4. Pray over your Goal List and see if there are any other tasks you'd like to write on your Monthly Lists.

5. Finally, write the Monthly Lists on full index cards. If you think of something you'd like to do this year but not every year, write it on a Post-it note and attach it to the appropriate Monthly List as a reminder. Store the Monthly Lists in the back of your chore card box.

6. Write a monthly chore card that says "Schedule a Monthly Planning session." Schedule your first Monthly Planning

session on your Family Calendar toward the end of this month.

7. Use Appendix A to guide you during your Monthly Planning times and Goal Reviews.

8. Spend some time lifting up a prayer of thanksgiving. Thank God that you are making real progress toward being the wife and mom He's calling you to be. Know that you're doing your best to walk in the path that He has laid for you, and that He loves you so, so much.

Chapter 8

1. Read the chapter and highlight anything that strikes your heart.

2. Pray over these reflection questions and spend some time writing out the answers to each of them:

   • Do you have a hard time keeping track of the information you keep on floating papers? How can you organize your thoughts and ideas?

   • Do you like your system for meal planning and grocery shopping? How could you use lists to improve it?

   • What other stores do you visit each week? Would you like to keep running lists for those places as well?

   • Do you have easy access to medical and homeowner information? What's the best way for you to keep track of these details?

- Do you carry spiritual clutter about borrowing and lending? Do you need a system to keep track of these exchanges?

- Is your list of birthdays and anniversaries up-to-date? Are there any new friends (or little family members) you need to add to your list?

- Do you have gift ideas for loved ones you'd like to write down? Would you like to keep a running Christmas List for yourself? Would this make you feel more or less contented with what you have?

3. Take some of the blank papers from the back of your planner and title them with the names of lists you know you'd like to keep there. (Or if you've printed the free Organizing *You* planner pages, get those lists out!) If you plan to keep some lists other places (in a folder or binder, on your computer, or on your phone) start those as well.

4. Decide where you'd like to keep your shopping and meal planning lists, and get them started.

5. Gather the information you need for lists like Medical Information, Homeowner Information, Items Borrowed or Lent, and Special Days. Write those lists.

6. Brainstorm about items for your Gift Ideas List and Christ-

mas List. Write those lists.

7. Review any sections you've highlighted and your answers to the reflection questions. Are there any ideas you'd like to add to your lists, or new lists you'd like to start?

Chapter 9

1. Read the chapter and highlight anything that strikes your heart.

2. Pray over these reflection questions and spend some time writing out the answers to each of them:

- Are there any fun, hobby-related lists you'd like to keep?

- What are some vacations you'd like to take? When would be the best time for your family to take them? What are some great day-trip destinations you've never tried?

- What at-home activities have caught your interest recently? Do you have wonderful memories from your childhood that you'd like to recreate with your kids?

- Are you writing down the funny things your kids say and do? Can you think of anything hilarious they've done recently that you don't want to forget?

- Are there any women in your life you'd like to get to know better? Are there any dear friends you haven't reached out to in a while? Who do you want to call or see?

- Do you remember to pray for people when they request it of you? Is there anyone you'd like to lift up now, and then put on a Prayer List?

- Have you leaned on different Bible verses at different times in your life? What are your favorite Bible verses right now? What is it about them that speaks to you?

- How would reading a list of blessings affect your spirit on a down day?

- Who are the unbelievers in your life that you'd put on your Most Wanted List—most wanted in the Kingdom of Heaven by you and your Lord? How do you want to remember to pray for them?

- Are there any other lists you might like to keep? What do you want to keep track of and remember?

- When and where do you get most of your ideas and to-do thoughts? Do you keep a notepad and pen there?

- Do you have a notepad in your purse already? How can you better use it to remind yourself about your thoughts and ideas?

- Do you ever displace objects? Does it work for you, or make you more frustrated? How else can you remind yourself of important things you'd like to do or remember?

3. Review the Chapter 9 list ideas, the sections you highlighted, and your answers to the reflection questions, and your Goal List. Then, as you did before, take some of the blank paper from the back of your planner and title them with the names of new lists you'd like to keep there (or get out the lists from the free Organizing *You* planner pages). If you plan to keep some lists other places (in a folder or binder, on your computer, or on your phone), start those lists as well.

4. Brainstorm about items for these new lists.

5. Look through your home office space or your special "pile" and see what you need to do with the pieces of paper you have lying around. Write as much information as you can in your daily planner and place the papers you do need exactly where you'd like to keep them (remember the wedding invitation example in Chapter 8).

6. Now that your lists are complete, decide how you'd like to order them in the back of your planner. Label each tab appropriately and put the lists behind each one.

7. If you have information you've decided to keep in a file folder or binder, place them where they belong. If you're keeping lists on different technologies, decide how you'll back them up so they're not lost.

8. Decide how you'd like to deal with ideas that pop up when

your lists aren't handy. Put a pen and notepad in all of your "thinking spots," and in your purse or diaper bag.

9. Review your Goal List to discern if any of your personal lists can help you reach your goals (see Appendix B for examples).

10. Spend some time in prayer asking God to reveal to you those things that clutter your spirit. Over the next week, really listen to the thoughts and ideas that pop up. Write them down as appropriate—as a new goal, a new to-do item, a new chore card, a new item for a Monthly List, or a new item on one of your personal lists. Clear out that spiritual clutter!

Chapter 10

1. Read the chapter and highlight anything that strikes your heart.

2. Pray over these reflection questions and spend some time writing out the answers to each of them:

   • Are you living with a cluttered heart? How can you demolish your anxious thoughts?

   • What thoughts get you down about yourself? Do you seek reassurance from your husband, family, friends, or other moms? How can you find the worth of your decisions from our Lord of Truth and within yourself?

- Do you have a favorite scripture for those times you begin to worry unnecessarily?

- What questions or phrases will challenge you to be realistic and positive about the work you're doing as a mom? How can you bring them into the light? What will it take for you to have a clutter free heart?

- Are you ready to continue this journey with Jesus? How can you continue to be intentional, realistic, and positive about the work you're doing as a mom?

3. Read over the list you made at the end of Chapter 1, the list of things you wanted to get out of this book. Is there any spiritual clutter you haven't tackled?

4. Take a piece of paper and write down any negative thoughts you carry about being a mom, wife, or daughter of God. (Yes, I know I told you not to do that.) Now, hold each of them up to God's Truth—are these thoughts true and right?

5. If the negative thought is true and right, write a new goal and decide how you'd like to use your organizational systems in order to take the appropriate action steps (as in Appendix B).

6. If the negative thought is a lie, lift it up to the Lord. Ask for His truth to redeem you, demolishing any lie and taking captive every thought to make it obedient to Christ.

7. Burn the paper.

8. Decide what verses, phrases, or reflection questions you want to use to guard your heart and mind in Christ Jesus. Try posting them all over your home and in your car for a couple of weeks.

9. Review the sections you've highlighted and your answers to the reflection questions. Is there anything else you need to do to clear out your spiritual clutter?

10. Consider how you'd like to continue clearing out your spiritual clutter. Do you want to write a monthly chore card or a to-do item on a Monthly List that will remind you to assess and clear out your spiritual clutter?

11. Spend some time with Jesus, thanking Him and asking Him to continue with you on this journey. Ask the Lord to fill you with His perfect peace. Amen!

Appendix A
Prayerful Planning

ORGANIZING
you

Daily Planning (allow 5 to 10 minutes):

- Check your Family Calendar for appointments and upcoming events.

- Open your planner to the correct day and write down any pop-up to-dos (and other useful spiritual clutter) on your to-do list, in your three time chunks.

- Assess your list and prioritize each to-do as a 1 (absolute must!), 2 (really want to), or 3 (wouldn't it be lovely?).

- Put a star next to your busywork items.

- Lay out the appropriate daily and weekly chore cards next to your planner in the three time chunks like a second to-do list (these are priority 2s and may also be busywork items).

- Pray over the upcoming day, dedicating it to the Lord and asking for His leading during the day to come.

Monthly Planning (allow 20 to 30 minutes):

- Gather your planner, Family Calendar, chore card box (with appropriate Monthly List), and shopping lists.

- Replace your planner pages, getting ready for the upcoming month.

- Pray over the upcoming month, thanking the Lord for all of the things to come and asking for clarity as you prepare.

- Review your Family Calendar, writing appropriate to-dos on your planner pages and adding to shopping lists as necessary.

- Review your Monthly List, writing to-dos in your planner, scheduling time for tasks on your Family Calendar, and adding to your shopping lists as needed.

- Place your monthly chore cards in your weekly Monday-Friday sections, matching like chores and spreading them out as evenly as possible.

- Choose a day at the end of *this* month to plan for *next* month and schedule it on your calendar (or write a to-do on the chosen daily planner page).

Goal Review (allow 45 to 60 minutes):

- Gather your planner (with Goal List and Greater To-Do List), Family Calendar, chore box (with appropriate Monthly List), and shopping lists.

- Spend some time in prayer, asking the Lord to reveal to your heart how He would like you to spend your time. Ask Him to lay on your heart the callings and desires He has for you right now. Pray for wisdom and clarity as you review your goals and the month that lies ahead.

- Review your Goal List and Greater To-Do List. Think through your relationships, personal dreams, and callings. Then write a new, current Goal List and Greater To-Do List.

- Review your Goal List and decide how to use your daily planner pages, note space, daily, weekly, and monthly chore cards, Monthly Lists, personalized lists, and God's Truth to their greatest advantage. (You may want to refer to the examples in Appendix B.)

- Assess your family schedule to make sure that your big chore days are still on the right days of the week for your family.

- Read through your chore cards to see if any of your tasks need to be done more frequently—or better still, if they could be done less frequently.

- Then, starting with your Family Calendar, complete the Monthly Planning process.

Appendix B

Example Goals
(and steps to achieve them)

ORGANIZING
you

I have to admit, I love Appendix B! These are some examples of how to use all of the planning tools at your disposal in order to reach your goals. This is where it all comes together to help you live intentionally in the abundance of Christ!

For each goal, write the first step on your daily planner to-do list. Then, consider how you can use your daily planner note space, Family Calendar, chore cards (daily, weekly, and monthly), Monthly Lists, your personalized lists, and God's Truth to be really purposeful about reaching your goals and forming new habits.

Example Goal: I want to grow closer to Jesus.

Planning Ideas:

- Write a to-do in your daily planner to get you started, like "Ask friends for Christian book suggestions."

- Use the note section in your planner to write down prayer requests or journal about moments when you feel especially close to Jesus.

- On your Family Calendar, make a date with Jesus—a special

time to spend with Him and pray over this goal.

- Make daily chore cards that say things like "Time with Jesus" or "Read one chapter of the New Testament."

- Make weekly cards that say things like "Thirty minutes of concentrated prayer time" or "Read one chapter of my new Christian book."

- Make a monthly card that says "Plan one service outing this month."

- On your Monthly Lists, write things like "Pray about observing Lent" (February), "Begin lunchtime devotions with the kids" (June), and "Choose three ways to grow closer to Jesus this Christmas" (December).

- Start a Blessings List, a Most Wanted List, and a List of Scriptures that are meaningful to you.

- Listen for any negative, untrue thoughts about yourself and how Jesus sees you—then find the scripture verses that combat those thoughts and post them in the places you'll see them most.

Example Goal: I want to be healthier.

Planning Ideas:

- Write a to-do on your daily planner page to get you started, like "Check out Weight Watchers Online" or any other research you'd like to do.

- On your Family Calendar, choose a date to check out a local gym.
- Decide to use the note space on your planner pages for a food and exercise journal.
- Write a daily chore card that says "Exercise" and one that says "Drink five glasses of water" (you can put it back in the box after that fifth glass).
- Make a weekly chore card that says, "Read one chapter of *Made to Crave*" (or another Christian "healthy living" book).
- Decide what day you'd like to "weigh in" and write a weekly chore card reminding you to do so. Or make a monthly chore card that says "Weigh in and assess progress."
- Make two Errand Day weekly chore cards that say "Put healthy food on the shopping list" and "Chop up veggies for snacks."
- Use your Grocery List and Meal Planning List to intentionally plan the healthy foods you're going to prepare and eat each week.
- Listen for your sabotaging thoughts (things like, *I've already blown it today so I might as well eat this,* or, *I'm stressed so I deserve this chocolate*) and decide how you want to use God's Truth to fight them—maybe with posted scripture, a positive phrase, or a written prayer.

Example Goal: I want to clean out the spare bedroom.

Planning Ideas:

- In the list section of your planner, make a list of small sections of the room to tackle one at a time ("clear off the bed," "get rid of the pile by the door," "clean out the top shelf of the closet," and so on).

- On your Family Calendar, choose a day and time to get started and schedule it like an appointment (this is a great "Project Day" task).

- Choose a section of the room from your written list to write on the daily to-do list for that day.

- When that day comes, just do it! Start by deciding what you want to keep, re-locate to another room, give away, and toss.

- Put the things you'd like to keep back in the space in an orderly fashion. Deal with the other piles appropriately, possibly by writing a to-do in your daily planner that says "Take donations to church" or writing "Have garage sale" on your May Monthly List.

- Then, choose the next day you want to work on this project, making an appointment on your Family Calendar and writing the next small section of the room you'd like to tackle on the appropriate daily to-do list.

- Keep going until it's done. If frustrated thoughts creep in, be sure to fight them with true thoughts like, *I'm doing exactly*

what I set out to do, completing this goal one step at a time,
or, *What's my hurry? I'm getting this done the right way and
I feel great about it.*

- You many need to write a weekly or monthly chore card
  that says "Pick up the Guest Room" to keep your work from
  going to waste.

- You may also want to make a note on your shopping list to
  purchase a décor item or two that will spruce up the room
  and give you some joy…and encourage you not to clutter it
  up again.

Example Goal: I want to spend less.

Planning Ideas:

- Write a to-do in your daily planner to get started, like "Research Christian financial planning books and seminars online" or other research you'd like to complete.

- On your Family Calendar, set aside a time to talk with your
  husband about budgeting.

- Decide to use the note space in your daily planner to keep
  track of your spending.

- Set an Errand Day to keep yourself out of the stores and
  away from impulse buys.

- Write a weekly chore card that says "Find coupons online"

(but only for things you were going to buy anyway!).

- Make a monthly chore card that says "Review spending."
- Write "Review Budget" on a few Monthly Lists.
- Start a Christmas List to hold all of your "I want" thoughts so you can let them go.
- Write a prayer or decide on a scripture to read before you enter a store and encounter all that stuff, focusing your heart and mind on the blessings God has given you.

A Step-by-Step Guide for Sorting Through Any Space

ORGANIZING *you*

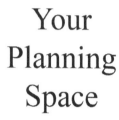

Your Planning Space

(on a nice busy day!)

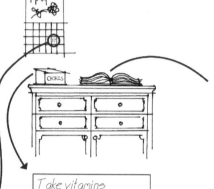

| Take vitamins |
| Exercise |
| Feed fish |
| *Weed flower beds |

| Friday, May 17 |

9-11:20 Preschool
11:30 Lunch w/ Sarah

6:00 Walters for dinner

Your Family Calendar
with time-sensitive items

| Devotions |
| Clean bathrooms |
| Clean kitchen |
| Wipe hard floors |
| *Dust |

| Check kids' backpacks |
| Vacuum |

Your Chore Cards
laid out in time chunks next to your planner

Friday, May 17	Appointments
	8:00
	8:30
To - Dos	9:00
	9:30
✓ Call Sarah to confirm lunch 1	10:00
Cut up veggies and fruit for	10:30
dinner 1	11:00
Wipe inside fridge 3	11:30
	12:00
	12:30
Make veggie dip 1	1:00
Make dessert 1	1:30
Sweep out garage 3	2:00
Iron tablecloth 2	2:30
Arrange centerpiece 2	3:00
	3:30
	4:00
Set table 1	4:30
Make casserole 1	5:00 Start making casserole
	5:30 Casserole in oven; start biscuits
	6:00 Walters arrive; biscuits in oven
	6:30 Dinner
	7:00
	7:30 Dessert
	8:00

Notes	Food	Exercise	Menu for Walters:
	Cereal	20 mins cardio	casserole
	Banana	10 mins abs	veggies with dip
	Yogurt		berry blend
			biscuits w/ jam
			dessert

Your Daily Planner Page

Chore Card Ideas

ORGANIZING
you

Daily Cards:

- Pray over the upcoming day, giving it to God
- Take vitamins/medications
- Take care of pets
- Devotions/prayer time
- Devotions/prayer time with your kids
- Exercise
- Pack lunches
- Take out trash
- Run or empty dishwasher
- Complete any tasks related to your job or career
- Check backpacks
- Sort mail
- Prepare dinner
- Have one and ONLY ONE piece of chocolate for dessert— Step away from the chocolate, Shannon! (Wait, I may be the only one who needs a card like this.)
- Pick up/straighten up
- Write in a diary or journal

The Big Five—Communication Day

Weekly Cards:

- Return e-mails
- Pay bills
- Check Facebook
- Call parents
- Correspondence (birthday cards, anniversary cards, thank-you notes, cards of sympathy and caring)
- Love up your hubby or kids with a note or special treat

Monthly Cards:

- Do a Relationship Check (through your address book and e-mail address book)
- Call or visit grandparents
- Invite a new friend over for dinner
- Invite an old friend out for dessert
- Check favorite blogs
- Plan a date night with your husband
- Plan kid date nights

The Big Five—Errand Day

Weekly Cards:

- Write a grocery list

- Run errands
- Take care of purchases
- Wash and cut up veggies and fruit

Monthly Cards:
- Clean out purse
- Clean out coupons
- Clean out car
- Wash the car
- Put new books and activities in the car for the kids

The Big Five—Laundry Day

Weekly Cards:
- Do laundry
- Iron
- Wash sheets

The Big Five—Cleaning Day

Weekly Cards:
- Clean bathrooms
- Clean kitchen
- Dust

- Mop
- Sweep

Monthly Cards:

- Dust ceiling fans
- Clean out bathroom drawers
- Wipe down cabinets

The Big Five—You Day

Weekly Cards:

None! Just a list of projects to complete in your planner… and a hobby or two you'd like to enjoy.

Monthly Cards:

- Renew prescriptions
- Get new contacts
- Do a breast self-exam

Other Random Chores

Weekly Cards:

- Water plants
- Reminders for kids (about practicing an instrument, returning school library books, allowances, trimming nails)

- Weed flower beds
- Mow the lawn
- Take that camera! (Look over the week ahead on your Family Calendar and note when you'd like to take photos or home videos)
- Plan a special at-home activity for your kids
- Check the fridge and pantry for old food
- Take the trash to the curb
- Pre-clean (A Family Whole-House Pick-Up the night before Cleaning Day)
- Plan a Family Fun Night
- Complete weekly Bible study work
- Prepare for the Sabbath (cook meals ahead, plan family fun and rest)

Monthly:

- Practice an instrument
- Review Goals
- Plan fun for upcoming holidays
- Back up any lists or other important information on your cell phone or computer

Remember, these are just examples! Decide to do what you want to do and how frequently you need to do it to satisfy your heart.

Appendix E
Monthly List Examples

ORGANIZING
you

Monthly Lists are really, *really* individual things, but this should give you an idea of what I'm talking about. Notice that some things appear only once a year, while others appear more frequently.

January:

- Sort through toys and find places for the new ones
- Replace furnace filter
- Wash inside windows
- Burn home movies on a DVD
- Schedule a Goal Review

February:

- Valentine's gifts/cards
- Fire drill/stranger danger
- Thoroughly clean pet areas
- Turn mattresses
- Start taxes

March:

- Upload pictures to computer and order prints
- Make Easter plans (outfits, baskets, coloring eggs, etc.)
- Check medicine expiration dates
- Bring a special lunch to the kids at school and eat with them

April:

- Call for mulch delivery
- Schedule summer checkups at the eye doctor and dentist
- Change the smoke detector and carbon monoxide detector batteries
- Sort through seasonal clothes and make shopping lists
- Put new photo prints in album(s)

May:

- Shop for warmer weather clothes for kids
- Buy end-of-the-year teacher gifts
- Clean up landscaping
- Plant flowers
- Have a garage sale
- Schedule a Goal Review

June:

- Make a new summer schedule and chore cards for the kids
- Have the kids write a paragraph about the closing school year
- Wash windows, in and out
- Straighten and sweep garage
- Clean out fridge and pantry

July:

- Replace furnace filter
- Wash all rugs
- Burn home movies on a DVD
- Check kids' toys for things they're not playing with

August:

- Dust high ledges, blinds, and woodwork
- Fire drill/stranger danger
- Take a special day trip before school starts
- Schedule a Goal Review

September:

- Make a new Fall family schedule and set new routines for the school year
- Call for absentee ballots
- Check medicine expiration dates
- Upload pictures to computer and order prints
- Sort through clothes and make shopping lists
- Bring a special lunch to the kids at school and eat with them

October:

- Put new photo prints in album(s)
- Change the smoke detector and carbon monoxide detector batteries
- Get flu shots
- Buy Halloween candy
- Choose dates for the Pumpkin Farm, Boo at the Zoo, and "Trick-or-Treating" at grandparents' houses

November:

- Clean up the landscaping
- Winterize around the house
- Start Christmas shopping
- Buy and address Christmas cards

December:

- Buy new planner pages
- Remember teacher Christmas gifts
- Wrap gifts
- Schedule days to get the Christmas tree, make a Gingerbread house, see Santa, and bake Christmas cookies

Don't forget to include reminders about your kids' birthdays, regular doctors' appointments, family holidays and traditions—anything you want to write down and let go!

Appendix F

Scripture List

ORGANIZING
you

Chapter 1: I Corinthians 14:33, Proverbs 14:1, Proverbs 14:8

Chapter 2: Ecclesiastes 3:1, Ecclesiastes 3:9-13

Chapter 3: Proverbs 16:9, Proverbs 16:3, Proverbs 14:22,
I Peter 5:7

Chapter 4: Colossians 3:23 & 24

Chapter 5: Exodus 20:8-11, Mark 2:27

Chapter 6: Psalm 4:8, Psalm 116:7

Chapter 7: Proverbs 31:17, 18, 21, 25, 27, & 28

Chapter 8: Psalm 112:5

Chapter 9: Psalm 91:1-4

Chapter 10: II Corinthians 10:5, Isaiah 40:10, Matthew 6:26 &
27, Philippians 4:6, Romans 8:28, Psalm 31:5, Philippians 4:8,
Isaiah 26:3

Afterword: II Thessalonians 3:16

Organizing You

Learn more about Shannon Upton's ministry or invite her to speak at your next event at www.OrganizingJesusMoms.com.

Here's what Christian moms are saying about Shannon Upton's Speaking Ministry:

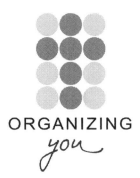

Shannon speaks to the heart of a mom by encouraging her dreams, supporting her with scripture, and loving the individuality in each mom's spirit. I left Shannon's presentation feeling like I'd just had lunch with a dear friend, and felt empowered to go into the "World of Mom" and make positive changes in my family!

Christy, mom of three and former MOPs co-coordinator

Shannon did a wonderful job! She was honest, interesting, funny, biblical, informative, and relatable.

Sue, MOPs mentor mom

Shannon has the knack for encouraging her audiences through tough topics that, in less skilled hands, might degenerate into frenzied to-do lists and a guilty conscience. Her presentations are well ordered and interesting, while Shannon herself is a charming blend of humor, common sense, and grace.

Kate, mother of two

It was a blessing to hear Shannon speak. Not only did I learn from listening to her, seeing it made me realize that this was something that I could do. After her talk, I was able to grow personally on my own as I read and reflected on the scripture references and questions she provided.

Elizabeth, mom of two and teacher

Shannon's presentation was entertaining and informative, well-organized, and full of practical tips. Her engaging speaking style held the group's attention, while her talk was encouraging and uplifting. I wish I had heard it when my children were young!

Christie, MOPs Mentor Mom

www.OrganizingJesusMoms.com

Made in the USA
Coppell, TX
16 November 2019